Jim a

Thank you for loving the children with us! ♡

Love,

David and Caroline

Dedication

To the One who opens His hand and satisfies the desire of every one of us.

The One God Brings

A story of surrender that ends in a marriage

By David and Caroline Webb

Introduction

We are writing to all the people who need hope and encouragement along the way to finding their perfect match. There is hardly a man or woman alive who won't relate to the youthful questions: What am I supposed to do, and Who am I supposed to do it with? We learned that these questions are intertwined.

Enjoy our story and ask God to answer your questions along the way. After each section, we encourage you to stop to think, to pray, and then wait on His answers. Our prayer is that your faith will be built to believe that God has someone who He made just for you!

David's Story

At Home in Africa

My wife and I are East Coast Americans, but we made our home in Africa. For more than twenty-five years of our thirty-plus year marriage, we have opened and operated children's homes in East and South Africa. We have fostered one hundred African children in our home. Our children's homes have cared for hundreds of children on their way to adoption. We had five Webb children, then adopted two more, then took in a "son-in-the-Lord" who we also cherish. We have seen dozens of miracles and hundreds of "God moments" that tell us of God's love for the children. It has been an amazing adventure.

How did our "Great Adventure" start? Through the years, many young people have asked us to tell our story. We don't start our story with the orphans, we don't start with marriage or even with meeting each other. We tell them how God interrupted our small dreams and introspection and gave us something to do that mattered. Most people know the deep desire to do something that matters, that takes your all, for all your life. Our journey was slower than we expected, and took some turns. In the end He got what He wanted.

My story starts with the ocean and with Africa and with God. But then He woke me up, and the pieces finally came together.

Growing up on the ocean

I remember my parents on either side of me reaching down to hold each of my little hands as another wave crashed over us and they hoisted me above their heads. They laughed and I screamed with delight. We all loved the ocean. As children we were told that Spain was on the other side of our ocean, which was on the East coast of Florida, and that we had better learn Spanish if we wanted to swim out really far. When I knew a little Spanish, I would swim out as far as I dared and scream "Hola" to anyone who might hear. I imagined village women on the opposite shore stopping and straining to hear. But the ocean was bigger than I imagined. It was more beautiful than my childlike mind could take in. It was like God. I loved the ocean. All my youthful memories started and ended there.

As a teenager I followed my brother who had a surfboard and who could drive before I could, and we went to the beach before school on many Spring and Fall days. I flopped around on his longboard long enough to admit that I would never be a surfer. I always said he had a surfer's body and I had a Polish farmer's body… an inheritance from our Polish mother's family. Still, I loved to go, I loved to be there, and I loved to feel salt on my hair and taste it on my lips at school the whole day.

As a young man I jogged on the beach, barefoot, for an hour each day. I didn't do it for exercise, I did it to feel the wind on my face, to feel alive in a beautiful place where I felt free and happy. Soul moments, for better or for worse, took me back there. The ocean was my first love.

As an older young man, I proposed to a spectacular young lady on the beach in a perfect setting with dolphins leaping across the rising sun. Later, I wondered if the joy I felt that day was just a mixture of sunlight and white powder and dolphins. I always knew that I would marry someone who made me as happy and as peaceful as I felt at the sea.

My love for Africa

My love affair with the sea was only rivaled by my passion for Africa. I left the United States and arrived in Nairobi at age 24 and stepped onto the tarmac in the middle of the April rains. I remember stopping in astonishment. The greens were greener than any green I had ever seen. The blue sky peeking here and there from behind the clouds was a rich blue. It was as though I had lived my life in a pastel version of the world but now I could see it for the first time. I thought, "I have been here before," but I knew that wasn't true. Then I remembered. It was the place I had seen in my dreams when I was a child, a place of vibrant colours. I had thought those dreams were of heaven. But now I knew. It was Africa. It was where I was meant to be.

I taught at a secondary school on the eastern slope of the Aberdare range, which was just west of Mount Kenya. Each morning, I would watch the clouds rise from somewhere in the valley below us, then envelope us in cool mist until they rose above us, often settling around the mountain for a bit, before dissipating or rising further or clinging to the summit. It was magical. I taught for a few months before accepting a job in Nanyuki that served northern tribal areas with education programs. After two and a half years of traipsing the northern parts of Kenya, from Marsabit to Baragoi to Loiyangalani, and after making hundreds of friends among tribal peoples and Italian missionaries, I knew I had to go back to the USA. I had no training to do the work that I now believed I was called to do and a master's degree, I was sure, was in order.

During my season in Africa, a college friend who was also doing volunteer work, who had a sympathetic ear and a gift for certainty, listened to my dreams and my hopes and assured me that I should move to Washington DC to study International Education or Development, where I had many college friends and where excellent degree programs could be found. She made so much sense... I found myself following her advice to the "t". After a visit home that turned into a long season, after an unexpected romance and engagement in my hometown in Florida, I found myself on track to get my master's degree in Washington, DC.

I had prayed for months that this was going to be a significant season. I had committed my life to Jesus Christ almost five years before. I had attended the Urbana conference and a speaker there said that even if you know Christ, you should re-commit tonight, so you will always have a moment when you are sure that you really did. So I did. I said a sincere prayer of repentance and gave my heart to God at 11:55 pm on 31 December 1981, New Year's Eve.

But now I felt I was further from God than ever. Sometimes, I thought, it is easy for a Christian to avoid God. Going to church and talking about God had become a substitute for knowing Him.

I prayed that I would find a great church where I would grow up and be a mature Christian. I knew what such a Christian looked like as I had mature Christian friends, and I knew that I wasn't one. I knew I wasn't likely to choose Christ over sin on any day of the week, and I was ready to end that season. I wanted to grow up.

I told God that I would visit a new church every Sunday for a year until I found the "perfect church." I often chuckle now when I hear of people in the middle of that quest. I know now that God does not need a year to put us where He wants us. When we are ready, he has it all figured out. We just need to go along.

On the way to DC I visited one of my best friends in Atlanta. He scribbled a phone number of a guy he barely knew who seemed to go to a great church and said "Call him, visit his church." Great, I thought, this will be the first of 52 churches. One down, fifty-one to go.

The Adventure: Washington DC

I said goodbye to the ocean and to my fiancée to start a master's degree in Washington, DC. The beach road was not the fastest way to start my journey north, but I needed to say good-bye to the sea one more time. I found it hard to believe I would be completely happy in a place with no ocean, but I mapped out the miles from my university to the nearest beach and planned to travel it often.

I stayed with a university friend in DC. That was one of the reasons I came to DC, to reconnect with old friends. But as often happens, the relationship was not the same. He was willing to help with a place to stay but he was very busy in a new job that he loved that was top secret and therefore he couldn't talk much about. Conversation was limited, and after one evening of reminiscing, it was time to part. Other friends were either off getting further degrees, taking jobs in other cities, or just too far away in a large metro area for my student budget.

All I had that first August morning in DC was a phone number and a determination to find God in a city with virtually no friends and very little money. I registered for classes at university surprisingly quickly, and picked up my textbooks in a matter of hours. I kept thinking of the phone number because what I really wanted was to start my God quest immediately. I called the number and talked to a very friendly guy who, when he heard I was at The George Washington University ("GW"), told me to come to his office, just a Metro stop away. He worked at a small publishing firm. I was there an hour later. "Hi," he said, looking very DC-ish in his pressed suit, cotton shirt and 80's paisley tie, "you must be David. Welcome. Come in. Have a seat." We chatted a bit and he brought in other staff to meet me… Stuart… Mark. It turned out they all went to the same church. It was the friendliest group of guys you would ever want to meet. Then they each shook my hand and said, "See you at church Sunday." I wasn't going to miss it. Years later I would marvel at God's planning. Each would be in my life for the rest of my life.

Finding the perfect church

On Sunday morning, I took the Metro to the DC Mall and found the hotel where the church was meeting, the Capitol Hill Holiday Inn.

I had the name of the ballroom where the church would meet, but on my way there, I passed another ballroom with a raucously loud band, blaring into the hallway. That ballroom also seemed to be in the middle of some kind of a church service. On a whim, I said, "I'll just stop here for a few minutes… maybe it is church visit number two." As I opened the door, I found myself in the middle of the most joyous and dynamic worship I had ever seen. Maybe it seemed that way because my dry heart was ready for a flood. I wondered momentarily if this was what heaven is like. Many people had their hands raised in the air and some were even dancing.

There is an image emblazoned in my mind of a young woman who suddenly started skipping all the way across the back of the room in a formal dress and stockings, barefoot, with her arms raised. Who was she? Why was she dancing? Why was she dancing where no one could see her? I instinctively knew the answer: she didn't want anyone but God to see her. I had been let in on a private moment with her and her Creator. She was dancing with all her might, but it wasn't for me or anyone else.

I already liked this church. I laughed to myself. "I think this is church number one after all." At the end of worship, Mark, one of the guys from the office I had visited during the week, hurried up to me. This was the church I had been coming to after all! He introduced me to his brother Kevin.

I can't remember what the sermon was about, but I remember thinking that these people were dead serious about Jesus Christ, and that was what I had been praying for. When the pastor called people forward for prayer after the service, I ran forward.

Pastor Mark asked how he could pray for me and I evaded the question, saying I wanted to repent of sin so I could be closer to God. He chuckled and leaned closer, conspiratorially. "Which sins?" I told him about my sinful sexual behaviour, what I was "really like." He listened, then said simply, "Not anymore." What did that mean?

There was silence. Then he burst back into the conversation suddenly. “You have a heart of unforgiveness! You have to learn to forgive if you want to walk with God!”

That made no sense to me at all. I hadn’t said anything about being mad or unforgiving. I wondered just for a moment if he had been listening. He said, “Raise your hands and pray after me!” I did, though the prayers he prayed meant nothing… I forgive my friends, my girlfriend, people who had hurt me accidentally and willfully. I felt nothing. And then he said, “and I forgive my father because he was never there for me.” As if breaking out of a trance, I lowered my hands and stared at him. There was excitement in his face. “That’s it! Raise your hands! You must say this.” He grabbed my hands and lifted them above my head.

I knew he had pulled something deep out of my soul that I had not intended to deal with that day. None of the first declarations was true but this one was unbearably true and hit a raw wound inside of me. I had harboured bitterness towards my father, and I couldn’t move forward until I had forgiven him. I choked out the words, “I forgive my father because he was never really there for me.” Then I burst into tears. Pastor Mark just smiled. “You’ll see. It will start to change now.” And he moved on to pray with the next person.

Dealing with memories of Dad

Memories of my father were always mixed. I understood that he was honest, faithful to his wife, a diligent provider who often worked three jobs as he and Mom raised seven children. But my childish questions to Mom about why he wasn't around usually brought defensive responses: "He's working." "He's making sure you get a good education!" All her answers sounded the same to me: "If I can raise a family without his help, you can grow up without him being around!" She was bitter and I learned her bitterness.

Much later in life I learned that he was a WWII veteran who came back from the war emotionally scarred. When he was in his 70's, I pressed in and asked him about his war experiences.

He was trained to be a radio-gunner in the SBD Douglas Dauntless. But when he arrived in the Philippines in March 1944, his Commanding Officer called him in and told him he was grounded. Apparently, he was the only man on the island who had also been trained to repair the radios on the Dauntless and they could not take a chance on losing him. To some, this would have seemed a tremendous relief: all day on the base and no immediate danger.

To him, it was a daily nightmare. Operating the ground radio, in communication with the radio-gunner, he would hear explosions, and "We've been hit." He would ask "How bad is it? Can you make it back?" He knew that if the answer was not forthcoming, that they were going down. His next words would be "Let's pray." He was raised Catholic, and he said the first time it happened, he prayed the "Hail Mary." Then he realized that most of the men were not Catholic, and he switched to the "Our Father." That is how my father came to spend the war on Green Island from a safe position, while he shared the last traumatic moments with dozens and dozens of US Marines. I believe a depression came over him in that season.

Ten years after the war he was still building his dream house with my mom and raising their first kids just a mile from his parents' home when his own father, whom he adored, attempted suicide. Later that night, his father died. My Mom said that in the following days Dad wept and that it was the first and last time she had ever seen him cry. The darkness settled in and he battled it for the next 45 years.

All this is to say that my father had reasons for being withdrawn and emotionally disconnected. As a teenager and young man, I did not know these stories, which had happened before I was born, and I had no patience for him. I became judgemental. But Pastor Mark said that I would grow up after I had forgiven my father, so I made up my mind that by God's grace, I would. At that time, I did not know the war stories, nor had I realized the effect his father's death had on him. Selfishly, I forgave him… for me. The fruit of an unforgiving heart was already having bad fruit in my life. I knew intuitively that in time, it would ruin me. I asked God's help, and something happened.

I had a moment where I saw my dad's brokenness and realized that it was not from bad character. It was from the weight of trying to do the right thing, decade after decade, while ignoring the hurt in his own heart. And yet all his good behaviour had not saved his comrades in the Philippines or his beloved father. There was a place he just wanted it all to be easier, but it got harder and harder. From that place, forgiveness flowed from me to him, and I could only ask God's forgiveness for what I had not understood and judged. I knew that even if he had just been a mean-hearted guy, I would have to forgive him, but God wanted me to know that in many ways, I was blessed to have a dad like him. I realized that although I had my own moral failings, I had gotten all my good traits from him. Years later I was able to honour him in a letter and thank him for the good character traits he had added to my life. He saved that letter, and I read it one more time at his funeral.

Church life – the good and the bad

I loved my new church, and I loved being around the people there. I was getting cleaned up from sins that had pursued me for years. Shame was lifting. I was happy. I sometimes looked for the girl who had danced across the back of the room that first day, but I wasn't sure who she was. Her face had been lifted to God, not to me.

Having recommitted my life to Jesus, I was asked if I would want to go to Ocean City, Maryland and be baptized in the sea during a church retreat. I chuckled; God knew me so well.

At the ocean, my new friend Kevin and a leader Eddie dunked me, while others cheered from the seashore. Sunlight, sand, white seagulls… it was perfect. I wondered again what it was that I felt, each time that I visited the ocean. I thought that maybe it is what I would feel like when I entered eternity. Everything else is put away… thoughts, worries, concerns. Everything disappears in the wonder of where I am.

But in the light of a new season, I began to feel strangely uncomfortable with… everything. My relationships… my career plans… my fiancée… my education. I was no longer sure that I was on the right path in any area. My days were divided between a new joy and a growing conviction that I was rudderless on the ocean of life.

Sometimes I thought of going to the airport, buying a ticket back to Africa, and leaving no forwarding address. I knew that my love for Africa would eventually take me back there, I just didn't know when.

When I heard that our congregation had planted a new church in a town near the sea in Williamsburg, I put my hand up immediately to go help and applied to a university near there. Somehow it all fizzled. My application was lost and the desire to move dwindled. I was learning new things in this remarkable church, and I hardly knew what to think about it. But I was convinced that God had led me there. I was learning to judge life and people wisely. Regarding my father, I had learned that I was no good at judging. It was good for me to sit and get good counsel and begin to be the person I had always wanted to be - a mature man in Christ!

The sermon that changed my life

One Sunday morning, Pastor Mark spoke on a topic that turned my world upside down. He said that God had known me, known every part of my soul, before the foundation of the world and that he had known my spouse then, too. If that was true, he surmised, surely He had "designed" our spouses to "fit" with us so that when He dropped us into history some millennia later, we would be just right for each other. Perfect in fact. I called the idea "interesting," and "startling" and I puzzled over it.

Back in my rented digs that I now shared with the brothers from my church, Kevin and Mark, I lay face-up on my bed which was my favourite I-need-to find-the-answers-of-life position. I stared at the ceiling, my hands clasped over my mouth, which thinking back was also the perfect posture. I did not want to answer my own questions but wanted to keep quiet and find God's answers. The weight of the matter hit me. How would I ever know if I was marrying "The One," the one who He had prepared for me. I remembered other parts of that day's sermon: He gave us the Holy Spirit so that we could always hear His voice. He does not hide from us. He answers when we knock. I thought I had heard already about who to marry. Now I was not so sure!

There were other parts of the sermon that day that seemed odd at first: ask your connect leader, ask your pastor. Don't move till they agree. To some in our congregation, that expectation seemed out of order. But as more than a decade of failed relationships flashed before my eyes, I warmed to the idea. I was faced with the hard facts of the sad romantic life of David Webb. I had almost 11 years of back-to-back relationships to prove I had no particular wisdom or discernment in finding "the One." I just could not figure it out. The idea that many people should advise and counsel in this most private moment was comforting.

And I trusted our leaders. I thought, "if I weren't already engaged, I would want to get engaged like this, with all my spiritual leaders in agreement." And it didn't matter what I thought of this new theory, I remembered. After all, I was already engaged.

The bed sank away from under me and my clasped hands moved from my mouth to my eyes. I was engaged… to a girl who was smart, creative, fun, balanced, and whose ancestors had attended church with mine for generations. The perfect match. My Mom was happy. My Dad was happy. We had never seemed to move to the planning stage, but we knew who would perform the ceremony, what we would wear, and that it would include the beach… for ceremony or reception.

I was engaged. I sat straight up. I searched for details that would assure me that she was, in fact, "The One." Nothing came. I liked her. I loved her. For the first time, I asked God, "Is she the one?" Silence.

That seemed odd. Hadn't I just heard that God wants us to hear His voice? I asked again.

And then my soul flooded with questions which I think came from Him: What was I thinking when I decided to propose? The honest answer was that I was getting old, 26, and I needed to settle down. Why had I thought she was the one? Answer: I liked her and she was the only Christian girl I knew my age in my church, and surely God had arranged that so I would be sure. How had I felt that day I proposed? I am old enough to do this; I need to grow up; I need to be responsible; buck-up, dude; wow the ocean is beautiful today; look! dolphins!

None of this sounded like the sermon I had just heard about how God wants to bless us with peace and certainty and joy at the One that He had prepared for us. The contrast was unbearable. As Mark Twain would say, it was like tasting gravel in a pie.

Studying Adam and Eve

I searched the Scriptures that Pastor Mark had used that day. The first story was the story of how Adam met Eve. In Genesis, God had made Adam and the Garden of Eden and told Adam that his life's work was to cultivate it. He set the man in Eden with a calling and resources to accomplish his call and only then, the Scripture says,
18 The LORD God said, "It is not good for the man to be alone. I will make a helper suitable for him (Gen 2:18)."

At that moment I would have imagined God in this great drama, waving his sceptre and causing a woman to appear fully formed from the cosmos. But there were surprising steps to this process.

First, God brought all the animals to Adam so that he could name them, finishing with the odd statement, "But for Adam, no suitable helper was found (Gen 2:20)." But surely God already knew that the animals were not suitable for Adam. What was the point? What was this exercise about with every single animal of the universe parading before God's appointed overseer, their master Adam? Then I got it.

God already knew. He needed Adam to know.

I have learned since then that men who are not aware of their need for a wife usually do not get one. I knew then (as Adam did) that I would never find an appropriate mate until God brought one to me.

The churning in the soul for a soulmate is a Godly thing, but it should move us to seek God, not a spouse.

Adam may have been completely happy with God and with his place in the universe, until the "name the animals" moment. Then the sad realization came over him: there is no one just right for me. There is a hole in my life and I can't fill it. Most men come to that sad revelation. Many men are surprised at the sudden realization, often between the ages of 20 and 35 but sometimes earlier or sometimes later, that they actually need a wife. I call this revelation, "the awakening."

Immediately after this humbling episode, God put Adam into a deep sleep. Through the years I have become convinced that the Godly place for a man to be, before

God brings him his wife, is asleep. Men who are out searching, trying to attract whoever is available, are neither safe nor trusting in God. They are relying on their list, on their wisdom and on their discernment. Women should avoid such men!

Women, on the other hand, frequently complain, "all the men in this church are asleep!" Thank God. Godly men usually are, until the day God wakes them up.

In Song of Solomon 8:4, the woman who sees that the man she loves is asleep, charges her sisters… "do not wake him!" Many women will try to awaken a man, through flirting and seduction, but a Godly man stays asleep.

When Adam was asleep, God took a rib from his side and fashioned a woman out of it. Same DNA. Same brain waves. Same values. Same heart. A perfect match.

The first woman had been a part of the first man. Neither of them would ever feel whole again until they were together. They would need each other.

We used to say at my church in those years that there is no perfect spouse, but there is a spouse who is perfect for you. The one who fulfils you, who makes you feel whole again, and who in turn feels whole when they are with you, is the one God made for you.

I realized that God doesn't need the help of men at all in making a spouse who is perfect for us. He needs us to sleep in that area and let Him do what only He is qualified to do. Let the God who formed our inmost parts and knows the substance of our being, figure out what we need. Our job is to stay out of the way. Sleep. He is on the job.

A day comes for every man and woman when they feel strange sensations, neither lust nor need, and can't sleep any more. They toss and they turn. This is good. God is nudging them, whispering "wake up." He is excited. It is time. He's bringing "the One."

"Then the LORD God made a woman from the rib he had taken out of the man, and he brought her to the man (Gen 2:22)."

It was God who brought Eve to Adam, and when Adam saw her, he said what men have said throughout the ages: At last!

Although all other verses in this book use the NIV version, I use the NLT version here because it captures the passion of a man in love… "At Last!" A man's heart leaps when, after a long, sometimes fretful wait, he sees that God has brought the wife that He has prepared for him!

At last! This is flesh of my flesh and she is so much like me! She really is the one! Adam knew it instantly and intuitively. Not all men are so fortunate. Often it takes a long second look… a sense of wonder, a feeling of confusion, and a determination to find out. Men who have been asleep find this season particularly difficult because they had already set their heart to stay asleep and wonder if this unexpected infatuation is a distraction and a waste of energy. Many Godly men start their first moments of awakening by rebuking "the awakening."

Thinking it through

Back on my bed, in my room, staring at the ceiling again, I was oddly peaceful, but I knew the pattern I just read about was not my life story. I remembered desperately searching for The One… a quick clinging to the one who fulfilled my current checklist… followed by a so-so relationship that needed constant bolstering to maintain. God's peace… nowhere in sight.
And I had done it again.

After I left my room, my roommate saw me and asked what I thought of the sermon. I told him I was blown away by it and it had caused me to think through my life. He asked if I would break up with my fiancée now. I was shocked at the thought. "Of course not," I said, "What kind of man would do that?" I was shell-shocked, but ready to marry the wrong one rather than "go back on my word." Even then I suspected there was some very misguided chivalry in my thinking, but I was not ready to admit it.

How does family history play in?

Like most people, I loved stories about how married people first met.

My father was stationed at the Marine Barracks in Washington DC in 1942 when his friend, Walter, invited him to spend their two-day leave in his hometown of Pittsburgh. They were both radio fanatics and Walter had worked at a Pittsburgh radio station, WCAE, and offered to give Dad a tour. Dad was excited. Arriving Sunday morning, Walter called his friend Jean and asked if she would call her cousin Virgie and go out to dinner with them.

Jean shuddered at the request but said yes. She shuddered because the night before, 28 November 1942, a fire at a Boston dinner club had left almost 500 dead. It was the only topic of conversation that morning and was on everyone's thoughts. She called her cousin who also agreed to come. As she was getting ready for the evening, city sirens announced a "blackout," a WWII phenomenon that endeavoured to make whole cities appear as no more than a small town, to evade bombers from above. It was probably, as usual, only a test but she dutifully pulled the blackout shades and kept only the smallest light on. When the doorbell rang, she ran down the steps to greet Walter Glaus and his friend, a farmer's boy from Florida, Bob Webb.

That night she was Walter's date and Bob Webb escorted her cousin Virgie. The talk was all about the Cocoanut Grove disaster. Mom looked around nervously, continually for fire hazards. But she liked the cute farmer's boy and was impressed with his manners and liked that he was a Catholic like herself. Somehow, they all agreed that they should go out again, and that Walter would escort Virgie and Jean would be Bob Webb's date. The rest, as they say, is history.

When Dad died on September 11, 2001 in his bed at home, all the talk that day was of the World Trade Towers attack. The paramedic who came to the house was the first to tell my mom what had happened. Mom later said to me, "It's funny, but my memories of meeting your dad are all wrapped up in memories of the Cocoanut Grove Disaster, and my memories of saying goodbye to your Dad are all wrapped up in the World Trade Towers. He came into my life during one national disaster and left me in a bigger one."

I once asked Dad how he knew Mom was The One. He said, I don't know that I did. I really liked her and she was interested and I kept following it up and hoping.

I once asked a pastor about this phenomenon of happy marriages that stand the test of time though the initial coming together was… uninspiring. I will never forget his words. "There is a lot of grace out there. If people are goodhearted and want what's best for themselves and the other person, God finds a way to bring them together."

When I was a child, my mother's mother lived in a beautiful house just across the street from the parochial school I attended. Every day after school, my brother and I went to Grandma Laura's apartment and spent the afternoon eating French crullers with fresh whipped cream from Denoel's Pastry Shop, on her best china with silver cutlery and drinking milk from crystal glasses. For me, even then a keeper of stories, it meant I had time to talk to Grandma about her life. Once, I asked her how she had met Grandad Joe. It was at a church dance. His Polish Catholic parish in Pittsburgh invited the youth from her Polish church in McKeesport to a big dance every year. There, they met. I asked her how they decided to get married. She just said, I liked him. He was from a good Catholic family and he kept asking me out.

My Grandmother Ruth was from a New York German family who moved to Florida for her father's health in

1911. She graduated from the same high school I went to 60 years later, a school run by the Sisters of St Joseph. She and her younger sister Helen had one bike between them and every day, one of them would walk and the other would ride for ten minutes. The one on the bike would get off and leave the bike on the side of the road and commence walking. The walking sister would walk to the bike and ride past her sister to an agreed-on spot, and so on and so on, until they were both at school.

In 1918 there was an air naval station on Anastasia Island, near what was called "Salt Run." Naval personnel manned the base and in 1918, a young sailor named Robert Webb was stationed in St Augustine. One night, he and his best friend Billy Wiler went into town and stopped at the ice cream shop on the corner of Hypolita and Bay Street. A pretty girl caught his eye and he sent his friend to find out who she was. Billy came back with her bio. "She's a German girl who lives out in the country." Grandma Ruth wasn't really German but her parents still had German accents from their immigrant parents.

Later that same week, Robert and Billy went to the local skating rink at the corner of St George and Hypolita. He saw the "German girl" and asked her if they could spend the evening with her and her friend, Vivian Bond. Shortly after, Vivian Bond married Billy Wiler and Ruth Schaller married Robert Webb. I asked Grandma Ruth how they decided to get married, and she laughed as if she had never been asked the question. I liked him. He had a good job. I knew he was in love with me. The twinkle in her eye told me the rest. She was in love with him, too.

I remember my Grandmother Ruth and my mother having a conversation once about what "young women these days" look for in a husband. They were shocked and puzzled that none of them seemed to care whether their husband was a good provider. They agreed that in their respective days, being a good provider was always at the top of the list or very close to it.

Although I remember asking my grandparents how their parents met, they didn't know. They guessed "at church, I suppose."

"At church, I suppose" was all the wisdom I had from my ancestors. I had, unwittingly, followed their example. My fiancée's grandparents had gone to church with my grandparents, and we found pictures of our grandmothers together at a ladies homemaker's club that met at my grandmother's house during the depression.

And still… was this God's perfect choice for me? Was she the one?

Studying Isaac and Rebekah

I remembered the second Scripture story that I had heard in Pastor Mark's sermon, the story of Isaac and Rebekah from Genesis.

Abraham was now very old, and the Lord had blessed him in every way. He said to the senior servant in his household, the one in charge of all that he had, "Put your hand under my thigh. I want you to swear by the Lord, the God of heaven and the God of earth, that you will not get a wife for my son from the daughters of the Canaanites, among whom I am living, but will go to my country and my own relatives and get a wife for my son Isaac (Genesis 24:1-4).

This story is almost unbelievable! Isaac had not been looking for a wife at all as far as we know! It was his father who was determined to have him settled. Perhaps Abraham was jumping the gun, but he had probably long been worried that his son would reach the age of marrying and choose from among the Godless people around them. If he waited, it might be too late to see him married to one of God's own people.

Abraham brought his most trusted servant and commissioned him to find a wife for Isaac. Abraham almost certainly knew what we learn from the story, that this servant feared God and would only do His will, and wanted only to faithfully complete the mission Abraham had given him. In this case, Abraham trusted God and the servant had faith that he could complete the remarkable mission… to find a wife for the young master!

The servant asked him, "What if the woman is unwilling to come back with me to this land? Shall I then take your son back to the country you came from?"

Make sure that you do not take my son back there," Abraham said. "The Lord, the God of heaven, who brought me out of my father's household and my native land and who spoke to me and promised me on oath, saying, 'To your offspring I will give this land'—he will send his angel before you so that you can get a wife for my son from there. If the woman is unwilling to come back with you, then you will be released from this oath of mine. Only do not take my son back there." So the servant put his hand under the thigh of his master Abraham and swore an oath to him concerning this matter.

Then the servant left, taking with him ten of his master's camels loaded with all kinds of good things from his master. He set out for Aram Naharaim and made his way to the town of Nahor. 11 He had the camels kneel down near the well outside the town; it was toward evening, the time the women go out to draw water.

Then he prayed, "LORD, God of my master Abraham, make me successful today, and show kindness to my master Abraham. See, I am standing beside this spring, and the daughters of the townspeople are coming out to draw water. May it be that when I say to a young woman, 'Please let down your jar that I may have a drink,' and she says, 'Drink, and I'll water your camels too'—let her be the one you have chosen for your servant Isaac. By this I will know that you have shown kindness to my master (Genesis 24:5-14).

Much like a young man in search of a wife, the servant asked himself, "how will I know?"

I related to that. I had been asking myself that question a lot.

He needed a sign. I needed a sign! But he could not expect his heart to beat for a young woman the way Isaac's might if he had accompanied him. He could not expect to have the opportunity to know the young lady's past and family circumstances as he ventured into an unknown land. He would have to trust God to show him. As he approached the well that day, he might well already have had a sense of wonder and excitement... the eligible ladies were already right there, as if waiting for an interview! But which one? Now, he realized, only God could help.

He had a spark of divine intuition. Are such moments really from within a man, from the mind of the person involved, or is the Holy Spirit actually telling the person what He is about to do? The thought came to him, that the woman who answered his request for water and who followed it up with an offer to water his camels as well, would be the one God had chosen.

Before he had finished praying, Rebekah came out with her jar on her shoulder. She was the daughter of Bethuel son of Milkah, who was the wife of Abraham's brother Nahor. The woman was very beautiful, a virgin; no man had ever slept with her. She went down to the spring, filled her jar and came up again.

The servant hurried to meet her and said, "Please give me a little water from your jar (Genesis 24:15-17)."

The servant went to the most beautiful young maiden at the well and asked for water. I can see Rebekah blinking in the sunlight. I feel sure the servant was a humble man and presented no threat. I feel sure her parents had brought her up well and she knew the importance of being kind to strangers. She said yes.

"Drink, my lord," she said, and quickly lowered the jar to her hands and gave him a drink (Genesis 24:18).

The clock is now ticking. The servant is waiting to see what she would do next, and what would flow out of the kindness that he had just witnessed.

After she had given him a drink, she said, "I'll draw water for your camels too, until they have had enough to drink." So she quickly emptied her jar into the trough, ran back to the well to draw more water, and drew enough for all his camels (Genesis 24:19-20).

Eureka! Halleluiah! On the first morning of his first day in the promised land, God heard the servant's prayer. I wonder if he dropped the water ladle and raised hands to worship. If he did, Rebekah didn't notice. She was busy watering the camels.

When the camels had finished drinking, the man took out a gold nose ring weighing a beka and two gold bracelets weighing ten shekels. Then he asked, "Whose daughter are you? Please tell me, is there room in your father's house for us to spend the night?"

She answered him, "I am the daughter of Bethuel, the son that Milkah bore to Nahor." And she added, "We have plenty of straw and fodder, as well as room for you to spend the night."

Then the man bowed down and worshiped the LORD, saying, "Praise be to the LORD, the God of my master Abraham, who has not abandoned his kindness and faithfulness to my master. As for me, the LORD has led me on the journey to the house of my master's relatives (Genesis 24:22-27)."

The kind of woman who says "I will go"

The servant astonishes her with gifts of gold jewellery and she takes him to her family's house. He delivers the whole story of his quest, and makes the outrageous request that they should leave in the morning. Naturally, the Mom is taken aback and the brother is worried. It is too fast. But a near cousin, Abraham's son Isaac, wants her hand and by the look of the gifts he has sent, it is a good match for her. At a standstill in the negotiations, they agree to ask Rebekah.

Then they said, "Let's call the young woman and ask her about it." So they called Rebekah and asked her, "Will you go with this man?"

"I will go," she said (Genesis 24:57:58).

Rebekah, a beautiful young woman, had probably looked around her village for some time and not seen the husband for her. She may have prayed and asked God to bring him from afar. But this was unexpected… a husband had not come from afar but the proxy of a clearly wealthy man has been sent and chosen her for the heir of all his Master's house. It was the ancient equivalent of a knight, or at least his trusty man, riding up on a white steed.

"I will go."

I will go. Here she echoes the words and the hearts of women throughout history, who love their families but know that they must go if they want their dreams to come true.

Now Isaac had come from Beer Lahai Roi, for he was living in the Negev. He went out to the field one evening to meditate, and as he looked up, he saw camels approaching. Rebekah also looked up and saw Isaac. She got down from her camel and asked the servant, "Who is that man in the field coming to meet us?"

"He is my master," the servant answered. So she took her veil and covered herself (Genesis 24:62-65).

When the servant tells Rebekah that this is the master's son, she quickly pulls a veil over her face. Today she is a bride, not a servant.

The kind of man who says "It's me"

Isaac took Rebekah immediately to the tent of his mother… the place of family. He let her know by this gesture that he fully accepted her as his wife.

We might feel all manner of confusion and puzzlement and even alarm. How could this possibly work? The father and his chief servant make a plan and Isaac must marry the one they think best?

But there was not another plan for how one got a wife. There was not a single book or movie to detail the emotion and uncertainty and rapture of a man and woman who find each other "on their own" without community assistance. This is how it was done. The grace of God can be found in many cultures and in many traditions.

As for their physical suitability, I once heard a pastor say that the beautiful thing about marrying as a virgin, male and female, is that our preferences are light and fleeting. In the act of marriage, they solidify and beat with the reality of the one they have wedded. This is the most difficult part of marrying as a non-virgin… our soul has already connected with another or others and the attachment there is… not unbreakable… but real and can shadow the marriage if not dealt with in prayer and counselling and ministry.

We know that Rebekah was beautiful and kind. But this passage gives not a single clue about Isaac's character or even his physique. But elsewhere in Genesis we see this is the man who, as a boy, had willingly lain on the altar to be a sacrifice to God. There is no record that Abraham chased Isaac around the altar and dragged him to it. He understood. God needed a sacrifice and he looked around and said, "it's me."

It's me. These words, not to be found in Scripture, are perhaps the most self-sacrificing words a man or woman can speak. It's me. Something has to be done, and there is no one else. There is no greater sense of calling than the realization that the Kingdom will only advance if I play the part that no one else will play. It's me. Simple and decisive. There is no record that Isaac cried and begged for his life that day. Maybe a shock, a momentary puzzling, and then he climbed willingly onto the altar.

Isaac was a great man and was fully submitted to God's will as it came through his father Abraham, long, long before the wedding season came and Rebekah came into his life. A trustworthy husband is one who has learned to say to God, "It's me."

The turning

One night soon after my first torturous battle lying on my bed wrestling with God, I found myself back there again, pondering the same questions. But this time, it all seemed clear. I felt a longing rise up in me that I had not felt before. God has a wife for me. He will prepare her and then in the right day He will show me who she is. All I had to do was to become the kind of man who followed after God with his whole heart, an "It's me" sort of man. I needed to forget the whole marriage search and become the man who trusts God with his whole life. All I had to do was wait.

The phone call with my fiancée was practically finished as it started. Two years of not progressing to the altar had made it clear to us both... we were not going there. At least, we were not going there together. She seemed... relieved. A melancholy sense of relief swept over me, too.

I hung up and stared out my bedroom window. It was the end of a season. It was the beginning of a new season. I was excited, but I was sad. Early December in suburban DC was dreary and though it was still early evening, it had been dark for hours.

All I had to do was to go back to sleep. And I did, first in the spirit and then in the natural. It was a long evening but when I finally slept that night, I slept more soundly than I had in years.

Single and waiting

My parents did not understand our breakup. I tried to explain to my Dad but it sounded too much like a religious fanatic had replaced his son, "I know God has someone else for me." How do you explain that?

I was later delighted with a line in the movie, "You got Mail," when the newly rejected significant other asks Meg Ryan, "Is there someone else?" After a thoughtful moment, Meg Ryan says, "No. No. But there is the dream of someone else."

This is the cry of millions of single people. It's not that the guy or gal in front of you isn't great, but somewhere deep inside we pray the heart will touch the soul when we meet our mate. This line has become a movie favourite. Every man and woman want their perfect match.

I became convinced that there were only two postures that would help bring my spouse: 1. Horizontal (sleeping) and 2. On my knees (praying). While sleeping, God prepares my spouse. In praying, God prepares me. Best of all is when you do both by turns. Both would position me to receive the woman God wanted to bring to me, but only when He was ready.

It was clear to me that I was not ready. What does it mean to be ready? In the natural, a man often thinks it means he has a job and a car. A woman often thinks she is ready when she has either found the confidence to believe that marriage and career can work together or has committed to leave the career when marriage to the right man presents itself. In general, a woman will change her whole life for the right relationship.

God's great secret

Only after I had let go of my plans for marriage, did He drop into my spirit an incredible secret. It was actually there all along but in holding onto my desires and plans, I had not seen it. God wanted something much more from my life than a happy marriage.

God wanted me.

It was incredible. With all my sins and bad character and misbehaviour, He wanted me. I would learn to stop striving to win God's approval.

I was never going to be perfect, but He wanted me anyway. I began to like parts of myself for the first time. I can be goofy when amused and I learned to like my goofiness. At other times I have a dry sense of humour that is often a mystery to those I love most. I learned to like that part of me, even when I am the only one laughing.

I have been fat and I have been thin. I have been generous and I have been stingy. I have been forthright and I have been secretive. I have been unjust and I have promoted justice. I have learned that I am awesomely and wonderfully made, and that God's works are wonderful. I knew it deep in my soul.

I smiled and said, "Clean me up Lord. And help me to sleep." I believed He would do both.

Thoughts on waiting

I began to ask myself, what do I want in a wife? God clearly wanted His best for me. I had realized that only a Christian woman would satisfy my heart and I knew that a non-Christian woman would leave me feeling lonely my whole life through, as I would never share that which was deepest in my soul.

But what else? I knew she would be pretty, though I had been around the block long enough to know that when you are in love, your beloved is always the prettiest girl around.

I loved literature and I felt sure my spouse would too. I envisioned long romantic picnics by the river and long nights by the fireside reading the classics, probably several nights of the week.

I knew my wife would be, NOT my mother. I loved my mother, but I knew I didn't want to be mothered. I wanted to be romantically in love with a woman who was like no woman I had ever met, who wanted me as a man and not as a boy. My wife would want to be my wife… not just to be married.

I knew what I wanted. I also knew that I was not yet the man for the woman I wanted. I said again, "Clean me up Lord. And help me to sleep."

My determination was tested once right in the middle of our church community. Here I was in a great Christian church where singles had agreed not to chase each other, not to search for a spouse, but to believe together that God would bring husbands and wives together in the right day. There was a girl in our church, a bit younger than me, who often chatted with me at parties and potluck dinners. She was kind and very interested in all my current problems, which she was determined to help me resolve as quickly as possible. I didn't know if she was being a great sister or a mother, but I was uncomfortable. I puzzled over it until I asked my housemate Kevin if he thought it was odd. He suggested I keep my head together and not to give any indication that I was interested in anything other than friendly chat. I followed his advice, even avoiding her once or twice. In a short season she had another new guy friend and I said, "well, that's that."

And I said again, "Clean me up Lord. And help me to sleep."

An even greater challenge arose as I began noticing a girl in the church who was fun, pretty and easy to socialize with. I made a beeline to her at every event. I was so grateful for a guy in the church who came to me and asked, "Has God shown you that she will be your wife? Because if He has not, then you are confusing her, or embarrassing her, or both, and delaying her finding the husband God has for her." I thanked God for friends who would speak the truth plainly and simply! I avoided her, too, and in a short season, found that I had forgotten her completely. That was a sign to me that God was not in it.

And I said again, "Clean me up Lord. And help me to sleep."

I heard stories of people who waited years... even decades.... for God to move but I didn't care. I was ok. I had a relationship with God that kept me warm, and I had plenty of my own issues to sort through. I enjoyed the season. I worked hard on my master's degree and made almost straight A's. I am embarrassed to say that the only "B" I made was because something fun was going on at the church and I skipped lectures to be a part of it. Every event having to do with the church grabbed my attention.

Once I was with my housemate Kevin at home and he was sick. A sister in the church called and offered to bring homemade soup. We were astonished. When Liz arrived with a huge pot of soup that would last our whole household for several days, she brought her sister Caroline who brought an equally sumptuous platter of homemade brownies. After they left, we sat at the dining table and laughed at our incredible blessings. Life was good. We were not chasing girls, but we had sisters in the Lord who treated us like kings… and like brothers.

An added bonus for me in my season of waiting was that I lived in Washington, DC. It was an exciting place to live. Everyone either worked in government or knew many who did. We were in the middle of history. I took a job as an administrator at the (old) GWU Medical Center to help pay for my university fees. My desk was one floor above the emergency room where Ronald Reagan had been treated years before after a 1981 assassination attempt. From my desk I could hear the sirens as presidential motorcades drove around Washington Circle, to or from the White House. I would run to the window, though only once was a passenger seat window partially open so that I could see President Bush Sr. as he passed. Sometimes the limousines were decked out with the flags of other countries, and we would find out from the newspapers who was on their way to see the President.

I briefly assisted Carol Laxalt when her husband Senator Paul Laxalt made an emergency appearance at the hospital and someone sent her to wait in my boss's office, in his absence, to await news. She was gracious and friendly even under stress though I remember fumbling her coffee while helping her understand how to use the office phones.

When Secretary of Defence Dick Cheney battled to get a hold of my boss and his physician Dr John LaRosa, I was appointed the go-to person and Mr Cheney had my direct line. I remember his always calm, fatherly voice, "Hello David. Dick Cheney here. Hope you are well (pause for my response). I'm glad to hear it. I'm hoping to speak to Dr LaRosa?" I always made sure they were connected.

I had the honour of working for Dr John LaRosa, Dean for Clinical Affairs, who was kind, smart and funny and adored his wife and children. Best of all, he took time to teach me life lessons. Once I responded to his near-impossible instructions with "I'll do my best." He looked puzzled, left, then came back to say in his best controlled fatherly voice, "David I know you'll do your best. Every one of us must do our absolute best every hour of every day. The world needs us all to do our best. But this has to happen today, and I know you'll have to knock yourself out to do it. So please, do it." He was later nominated for Assistant Secretary of Defence for Medical Affairs. He turned down the nomination after considering the undue pressure on him and on his family. I admired him deeply.

A church friend gave me and my housemates tickets to hear President Ronald Reagan speak at the DAR hall. It was memorable.

I often feel for people whose season of waiting is not fun or exciting with new people and new things. I understand that some will sit and stare out the window wondering, "when, O Lord?" I believe it is important to hang around people who are like-minded, who are also waiting, who have a conviction of God's faithfulness and an attitude of faith. Beyond that, I only know that steadfastness is a virtue. Faith pleases God. Your waiting is a story of faith. Let it be one that will inspire the generations!

God starts to wake me up

Sunday!! This was my new favourite day of the week. Always up and at the church quite early, I helped move and set-up sound equipment at the Capitol Hill Holiday Inn. I looked around. It was an all-single crew of men who believed, like me, that God would show them who to marry. I was living with a true band of brothers. I knew that many would one day hear our stories and pity themselves that they had not been here. It was a place where everyone I knew was trusting God for something, either for marriage or for peace that marriage was not God's will at this time or for a great career in preface of marriage. For most in this 20's-something group, it was marriage.

The day before there had been a wedding in the church. In retrospect, I should have attended. I was verbally invited by the prospective bridegroom but my hunch was that the invite was a kindness to me as the new guy and I did not believe I was wanted there when I knew almost no one. I said no, so Brett and Cynthia were married in a beautiful event with almost all the church except me. As Brett and Cynthia became dear friends and mentors in years to come, I often regretted saying no. But I used the evening well, closing out my last season in prayer and asking God to make me the man He wanted in the new season.

Pastor Mark surprised us at church the next day, Sunday, by saying he would not preach. I later heard him explain that everyone was exhausted after the wedding and he just wanted to encourage people. Instead, he called up person after person and gave them a "prophecy" from his mouth but, we charismatics agreed, were actually an encouragement from the heart of God. Most of the people who were called up I did not know yet. There was one that I did know, Liz Grabau. She was in my home cell and I had taken the subway with her from Capitol Hill to Arlington after meetings. The pastor called up "The Grabau sisters," Liz and Caroline. I remembered them then as the soup and brownie sisters.

I don't remember what Word he gave Liz, but the Word he gave Caroline burned in my soul in a way I could not explain.

"Caroline, you have the heart of a mother. You have the same heart Jesus had when he said, 'Suffer the little Children to come unto me.' He has given you that heart because he is bringing many, many children to you. First there will be your natural children, but after that there will be many others. Many children need the heart of Jesus and you will bring it to them. Even children of other nations will call you mother."

Something was exploding deep inside of me. I fought back tears, but I did not know why. With a shaky voice I nudged my roommate and said, "that was beautiful." He looked mildly touched and said, "Yeah, that was great." I couldn't contain myself. My mind was spinning. I sobbed. Then I thought, "It is my prophecy too." I had heard of that… sometimes you feel someone else's prophecy strongly because God is speaking to you, too. I sat straight up with my head above the crowd so I could see this amazing woman of God when she came back down the aisle. Red blouse, Khaki skirt, modest flats. So that is Caroline Grabau.

I said in my heart, "Dear God, give me a wife like that one day."

I thought little more about that moment except that I held Caroline Grabau on a pedestal above all other women in the church from that day. In the months that followed I realized that everyone who knew Caroline had her on one sort of pedestal or another. "Where she rightly belongs," I thought.

The revelation at Bible Study

On New Year's 1987, I attended my usual home cell group. Our leader spoke about the things God wanted to give us in the year and years ahead. He showed us in Scripture what happens to people who take delight in God:

"Take delight in the LORD, and he will give you the desires of your heart." Psalm 37:4

He taught us that some scholars suggest this means, "He will put desires in your heart." He will give you the desires so that you will know them and rejoice when he fulfils them. But sometimes we haven't discovered the desires which God has put in our heart.

Our leader said, take a moment and pray, and ask God to show you a desire in your heart that you did not know about until today, that He intends to fulfil.

This was a novel idea but we had the Holy Spirit so I believed we could hear a new thing, right? I prayed and after a moment, I knew.

We went around the group sharing what God had shown us in that moment of prayer. I said, "God showed me that children are going to bring me a lot of joy." People were fascinated and asked me what that meant. I said, "I don't know, I guess that means I'll have a lot of children. One woman asked, "how many is a lot?" I shrugged my shoulders and said, "twelve?" Many people laughed, a few looked dumbstruck.

The conference

About a year later, our congregation was asked to manage children's ministry at our regional conference, and everyone was asked to sign-up for a volunteer slot, so of course I did. I had a note with the hotel room number and time I would serve. I was to serve with another church member and have up to six children in the room. When the time came, I appeared at the room. The occupants of the room said, "Good, you're here," and ran out the door for the conference. When the first parents came, I said, "My helper is not here yet, but you are welcome to leave your kids now if you like." They did. So did the next couple, and the next couple. And the couple behind them. Each couple looked at their watches and mumbled something like "I'm sure it will be alright," as they raced to find seats in the unreserved seating conference. In the end I had 12 children and two of them were under two, so

I carried and bounced them. After a while there was a knock at the door.

I opened the door to find Caroline Grabau, Children's Ministry Coordinator. My heart melted. "How is it going, David? You have a lot of kids here, "she said, looking past me. "Where is your helper?" I explained that the other volunteer had not shown up but that we were all ok. She looked at me with wonder. "You have twelve kids here but it's ok?" "Sure," I said, "the babies need holding but the others are kids are fine… self-supporting…. amusing themselves." She sized up the situation and said "Well, I am supposed to be free to supervise but this is way too many in one room. I'll take all the girls, and you keep all the boys." "Sounds great," I said. "I can help you get as far as the elevator, where I am still in hearing of the boys in my room, but then I will have to turn back."

As we walked half a dozen girls to the elevator… including both babies… I said to her, "Wow Caroline, seeing you with all these kids… it's just like the prophecy you had at church!" She looked puzzled.

"You remember… Pastor Mark said you had the same heart that Jesus had when he said, suffer the little children to come unto me." I could see that she was remembering.

"He said that He gave you that heart because many children are coming to you, in the natural and the spiritual, who need the love of Jesus and you will give it to them."

She was silent. “He said that even children of other countries would call you mother.” I loaded the kids into the elevator and gave her a wave as the doors closed. She didn’t say anything. I guessed she was too busy with the kids for chitchat.

It never occurred to me that I had recited to her verbatim a prophecy that she had received more than a year before. I didn’t know Caroline Grabau at all, but I was fascinated by her and season by season kept her on that pedestal in my heart. It never occurred to me in that season that this was odd. After all, everyone who knew Caroline adored her.

It was a great season because God used it to clean me up from sins and attitudes and judgements that had held me back. A few times I was rebuked by my leaders. I hated it at the time but I understood that God disciplines those whom He loves (Proverbs 3:12). Loved. I still did not like “father figures” but I understood that Father God was different. He liked me. He loved me. My heart melted often in that season. I cried more at movies, at melancholy poems and often at church. Opening myself up to God had made me softer, kinder, and more sensitive to other people’s plights. I thought often of the Scripture, “I will remove from you your heart of stone and I will give you a heart of flesh.” (Ezekiel 36:26)

And He gets us ready so that we don't hurt the One that He is preparing for us. I often thought at those moments, thank God I am not married yet because my wife would have to be part of this.

Lust was a problem. I learned that if you confess your sins, that He is faithful to clean you from the unrighteousness. How many times? Every time. Never is there a time he resists reconciliation. We resist in our shame and pride, but He never does! I learned that there was a good reason to have Christian roommates. I learned there is a good reason never to be out after 10 at night. I learned that the simple old-fashioned rules generally work. Don't act like you're interested if you're not. Don't flirt (a sign of physical attraction) unless you think he/she is the One and you are on the path to marriage. Respect always. Off-colour jokes are too often disrespectful to women, which is never ok. I learned to love cold showers. I learned to distract myself with good things… a legitimate way to learn self-control!

I continued to be very active in our church and that included serving in the campus ministry. I was fortunate that although I could barely explain my faith, I had Dawson and Anne, our church campus leaders, to be patient with me, to teach me, to encourage me. Dawson sat me down at the University cafeteria and taught me step by step how to tell someone about the Lord. After a season we had an international Bible study that met every

Tuesday night. It was tough to get room bookings on campus but a member of the church, Marie, lived just two blocks off campus and let us use her apartment. It was a small group at first but in a short season there were 30 of us squeezed into that apartment. We asked for people from church to attend and several started coming to help. A few weeks after that, I had a call from Caroline Grabau asking if we still needed help at the study. Honestly, I said, not now, because several new people are coming but thanks for offering.

Shortly after she asked me if I could take a Sunday shift at the children's church. I said no, because I often was bringing students to church and that would interfere.

Campus ministry

A month or two after that, Caroline began attending our campus Bible study. I learned that my co-leader Laurie had asked her to come and help her with the ladies. I was glad to see her but a little embarrassed to lead the study, knowing she would be there. What would she think? Was I up to her standards?

I often led the Bible study. Church members saved the day by answering my questions as the new or not quite yet Christian students were shy or unsure of the lesson. Caroline always did her part. I began to love the simplicity and the depth that always rolled from her heart.

Afterward, there was time to socialize, and I began to appreciate her even more. She was a Godly woman, full of faith, always ready with a wise word.

I also knew that she barely knew that I existed. I would pass her at church and half-step into her path to get her to say hello and she always said hello as though she was struggling to remember my name. "Hi Caroline!" She looks up as though disturbed from deep thought. "Oh hi… David." At least she remembered my name.

Then one Sunday, I saw Caroline skipping across the back of the room in stockings and a dress in abandoned worship, and I realized… she was the girl I saw when I first walked into this church two years before! My first image of this amazing season was Caroline Grabau.

Confusion along the way

I began to really look forward to Tuesday night Campus Bible Study. Once, I left my car at home and took the metro to downtown DC. After the meeting, I mentioned to the group that I was headed back via the Metro and Caroline said, "Oh I can give you a lift home. I know where you live." Of course… the brownies.

Washington is beautiful at night. Much of it is a stunning wonderland. But as we drove through the streets, our talk was all of the Bible study. Caroline would begin, "What the students didn't understand was…" and I would finish her sentence. She would add "Because God always…" and I finished her thought again. I said, "What they need to see about God is that…" and she would finish my sentence. I had a thought that this is what old married people do… they finish each other's sentences because they think so much alike. Finally, I just let her talk because her grace and wisdom and simplicity had me… completely charmed. Just charmed. I just wanted to hear her thoughts. I just wanted to hear her voice. I don't know how long we had been sitting at the foot of my driveway before I said, "Well, I should go now. Thank you." I wandered up the driveway staring at the ground asking myself, "What just happened?" It was a Twilight Zone moment. As I walked, I turned around and saw Caroline still sitting in the driver's seat, looking at me. I burst out of my trance to say happily, "Good night! See you Sunday! Thanks again!" She startled out of her trance and said, "You're welcome! See you then!" And she was gone.

I was in trouble. I had promised God that I was through with chasing girls, but I knew I really wanted to chase this one. I would have to be extra careful and not let my heart get out of hand. I said this but I knew… I was already in trouble.

Next week, I left my car home again. I have no excuse. I knew there was no other end to the evening except that she would offer to give me a ride home. And she did. The moment was not so dramatic, but a connection was growing. She definitely knew my name.

The next week I drove my car downtown for the Bible study. Sitting in a parking spot outside the apartment, I suddenly realized what I had done. I had driven myself to Bible study. I was panicked. Was there time to drive home and take the subway back? No. Definitely not. I began to pound the steering wheel while rebuking myself.... "You stupid.... thoughtless.... I can't believe you..." But there was no way to fix it. I went sadly into the Bible study. Later I drove myself home, deeply disappointed.

Still, this was fun. I liked being "in like" with a girl as great as Caroline. I also knew that if I even said her name aloud to my roommates, they would probably line up and take turns rebuking me. Caroline Grabau was deeply loved by pastors, guys and girls alike in our church. I knew my place. I was still the guy who had walked in off the street for deliverance two years before. Still... I was happy. She knew my name.

Our weekly chats at Bible study or at church events were highlights of my week. I ventured out a bit and asked about her family. Once, with her sister present, I asked, "So where are you all from?" Equally confident, Caroline said "Vermont" while Liz said "Connecticut." Then they looked at each other and burst into laughter. They had been brought up in Connecticut but in their teen years after their parents' divorce, they and their mother had moved to Vermont. Liz still had a heart for their home state where she felt she belonged and to which, some years later, she would return. Caroline had fallen deeply in love with their adopted state of Vermont, with its beauty, its good-hearted people, its simpler and quieter lifestyle. So, Liz was from Connecticut, but Caroline was from Vermont. They were deeply attached to their mother and brother David. David had left to pastor a new church in Williamsburg two years before. His was with the church whose proximity to the sea had almost lured me to leave Washington just after I arrived. I mentioned this to Caroline and she said that she had almost left DC at that time to help her brother plant the church. I thought to myself, so if I hadn't met you here, I would have met you there.

I still remember one event when we laughed and giggled and told stories… just the two of us… but in a crowd of people. I can't remember the place or the reason for the gathering. In my memory, we were utterly alone. She wore a turtleneck sweater and an uncharacteristic amount of makeup and jewellery. It must have been a special occasion but for me, it was just the two of us. I remember people moving all around us but no one interrupted. Probably, people began to wonder that night about David Webb and Caroline Grabau. Just as I was wondering.

The following Sunday I raced to church, happy as always, looking forward to seeing Caroline. But she was not there. I was on usher duty as usual but though I lingered and looked long down the hallway, she was not there. Worship was over and it was time to take our seats, but she was not there. I wondered what had happened. Was she sick? She told me that she was never sick and so it must be a pretty bad sickness to keep her from church. Maybe her sister was sick. I wondered if she had a flat tire. I remembered that it was raining and thought she might be out in the rain changing a tire. For a moment I wanted to leap from my seat and go find her. But I restrained myself. Afterward, I asked one of her friends, as casually as I could, "So where are the Grabau sisters today?" I didn't want to give myself away by asking after Caroline, so I thought "The Grabau sisters" was a good cover. "Oh, they went to visit their brother David in Williamsburg."

I was stunned. First, I was relieved, then astonished, then angry. How could she go away and not tell me? We had just had that long, lovely conversation, all alone, and shared all about our lives. How could she not tell me that she was going away?

On balance, why would she tell me her private movements? We were just friends who attended Bible study together. I was nobody to her. And then I was depressed. And I realized then that I might be losing my mind. This went on the rest of the day... confusion... anger... depression. I wanted to talk to someone, but no one knew that I had created a whole unfounded world in my mind with a sister in the church. There was only one answer. I had to talk to God about it.

Talking to God and to Stuart

In the last years I had learned a lot about hearing from God through His Holy Spirit. I had heard many Christians use the phrase, "God spoke to me that..." It made sense to me. I knew that God was not hiding from us and that He would certainly want us to know His plans for us. I knew that if I asked, He had an answer. But in reality, I had no experience of it. I had tried to live in a Godly way these last two years as my conscience and common belief dictated. But what is this, "hearing from God" really all about?

I prayed. Silence. I prayed again. Silence. I told God he had to forgive me for the infatuation I had developed over this girl and to "heal" me. Silence and I was still infatuated with her. I asked Him if she and I had a future together. Emphatic silence. And still I never doubted that God could speak to me. He just wasn't. Or I wasn't hearing. I confessed my many sins again in hopes of "clearing the air." The silence was deafening.

I had to admit that I had never heard God's voice in my life and wouldn't know what He sounded like if He shouted in my face. I decided to do the next best thing. I would talk to my best friend about all of this.

I delayed. Fear of rebuke or that my feelings were unfounded haunted me. Then I stopped doing my schoolwork. In my last semester of a master's degree, I spent long hours staring at my books and staring out the window and doing nothing at all, except thinking about Caroline. I was in serious doubt whether I could finish my degree. I tried other study venues to break the mood so that I would get back to studying. I went to the Reading Room at the Library of Congress where I had spent a semester writing my thesis. I went to the campus library, where I had never studied, and found my heart palpitations following me. I was in so much trouble.

One Fall morning as I was driving Stuart to work… I don't remember why as I did not usually drive him to work… I asked him to pray for me because I had stopped doing my work. He was puzzled. He asked why? I said I was thinking about a girl all the time. What girl, he asked. I burst out over-loudly, "Caroline Grabau." He was calm. I was distraught. He said, I certainly will pray for you. God gave you a good mind and you have done very well in your Master's work. I will pray that you start working. But one more thing. Could this be how God talks to you? You are old enough to get married and so is Caroline. You are about to finish your master's degree. This would be a good time to get married. I was incredulous. I fought back tears. Fortunately, I had to keep my eyes on the road so he couldn't, I hoped, see my reaction.

He said, you need to set a season to fast and pray about this. God will let you know. I committed that as soon as my studies were over, I would fast and pray. That gave me three weeks to finish my schoolwork.

And that is what happened. Incredibly, I forgot my heart issues and worked all-out, day and night, for three weeks. Just before 5 pm on a Monday evening I placed my last paper in the "due box" attached to my professor's office door in Building C at the George Washington University, and walked out, knowing that I was finished my degree work. I was very glad to be done. But I was very glad to be on to a much more important thing. I was ready to fast and pray.

A short fast and an answer

I had seen Caroline at church and said casually, "hey we missed you and Liz. I heard you went to see your brother?" She was brimming with excitement. "Yes! He got engaged and he wanted us in town so we could be part of the church announcement!" I asked all about it and kept thinking… it should have been me. I should have gotten engaged. I was adding jealousy to my list of sins. At that moment, I really didn't care.

I listened with real interest, thinking how beautiful she was when she was happy… which was pretty much all the time.

I knew nothing about fasting except that I couldn't eat. For five days I ate nothing. The fifth day was a Saturday, and I had been invited to a friend's house for fun and hanging out. It was just a pleasant time of playing pool and board games while some were watching a movie. I told people that I had a stomach ache and couldn't eat. Oddly enough, that was absolutely true. By the time I got home I had a serious case of the flu and a fever to boot.

In the morning, I got up at my usual time but only to call our set-up team leader and tell him I was sick and wouldn't be at church. I decided to eat some crackers and have some hot tea and decided that my fast was over… that I needed to focus on my health. I was really sick. I took a long nap and had a dream. I was back at the ocean at night and the stars were beautiful and I was happy.

A moment to last a lifetime

After this long nap I got up and pulled out my Bible.

There are moments that last a lifetime. This would be one.

In my mind I can see the room as it was that day… the furniture that I bought from the homeowners when they moved out. The room painted cream with white trim and green bushes outside the high windows (it was a basement apartment), the bed linens and their pattern. I remember it all. And I began to pray.

Dear God, I need to know about Caroline. I am sick… I don't care about anything today really. Not work, nor church, nor my future, nor who I am to marry, but I need to know. Please answer.

What flowed through my mind at that moment was almost inexpressible. All the thoughts, looks, moments, wonderings of the last months passed through rapidly. But the feelings that I had in every moment was the same. In modern language I might just have said, "I love her." But it was more than that. I wanted her by my side. I wanted every moment to include her. We were already part of each other. Her soul and my soul were meant to be one. I knew it. I knew that being sick or having a bad day or being unfocused would never change what I knew. She was made for me.

I heard God's whisper, "I have been telling you for a long time." How much gentler and how much more fatherly were these words than the "yes" or "no" I had expected!

I have often heard church people say that when seeking God, there is a moment when you know that you know that you know that you know… that you have heard Him.

I knew. I really knew. And I began laughing. I laughed and I cried.

I knew that I could hear God's voice and that He had just spoken to me. It was the gentle whisper (1 Kings 19:12). It wasn't my voice or my family's voice or my best friend's voice or my pastor's voice. It was His voice. I have learned that half the secret to hearing God's voice is being sure it is not any of the other voices that run rampant through our minds.

His voice didn't come by a Scripture as I had thought it might. I would have liked a Scripture to jump out of the pages of my Bible. I told God that I liked hearing His voice and though I had expected to hear this news in a Scripture verse, I was happy and excited that He had chosen to speak to me.

I looked up. The room seemed brighter, the cream walls almost yellow, the trim a brighter white, the green bushes outside the window greener, the sunshine brighter than I had ever seen before. I knew.

I opened my Bible, intending to be faithful to my daily reading, but instead let the Bible fall open and I began to read:

"… may you rejoice in the wife of your youth. …may her breasts satisfy you always, may you ever be intoxicated with her love.' Proverbs 5:18

I was going to marry Caroline Grabau. She didn't know it yet but God knew it and I knew it and it would be our secret till He was ready.

I was fully awake.

I wondered if this incredible revelation is what my Christian friends meant when they said, "I heard from God." It was life changing. I wondered if it might be possible to hear from Him again like that in my lifetime. I had gone from living on hunches of God's will to an intimate hearing in a moment. Could there be more to knowing Him than I imagined?

In years and decades to come, I found I would rely on hearing His voice every day of the week, and sometimes many times in a day, as I first heard Him that day. I remind my brothers and sisters in the Lord regularly that it is our heritage as born again, spirit-filled Christians that we can hear His voice. He helps us to hear Him; He wants us to hear Him. He never hides from us. He asks only for us to press in and wait. Part of the waiting, as I said before, is to be sure that once we have heard His voice, that we know the sound and can distinguish it from every other voice that speaks to us. I found that the hardest part of hearing His voice was to drown out the many other voices: my voice of "I should," my voice of shame, my voice of regret, my voice of manliness that was only a thinly veiled pride in myself and had no place in obedience to Him. All these voices screamed loudly to get my attention and demanded my heart's submission. God's voice, when it comes, is like a gentle wind and all other voices must be denied before one hears it. Knowing what it sounds like is worth everything.

After a God moment

It is hard to act normal after a God-moment. I was supposed to go to a carolling party at Caroline's house that night. I pretended that I was better and went, feverish and dizzy. At the party, I saw Caroline and plopped into a comfortable stuffed chair, unable to move due to sickness and exhaustion. Shortly after, everyone was ready to go carolling but I knew that I couldn't. I could barely walk. I said, "I'll just wait here and rest till you all get back. I've been sick and I need to rest." Caroline, ever the hostess, said she would get me a hot drink and something to eat first. I wanted to beg her to stay but could think of no reason other than that I wanted her to stay. She left and I cried, fuelled by the emotions of the day and by my complete exhaustion from being sick.

When I next saw Caroline at Tuesday Bible study I smiled broadly and said "Hi, Caroline, how are you?" But I knew there was a confidence in my greeting that had never been there before. After the students were gone, we chatted in the kitchen. I asked how it was going with her brother David and his fiancée Maia. There was no jealousy in it. They were happy and I was glad for them. And one day soon I would be married, too. I wondered when I might get to meet David's fiancée. I knew who he was by reputation and that he was the famed Grabau brother I had heard so much about. I remember from one brief meeting at a conference that he was kind and a good conversationalist. I was eager to meet Maia.

During this season Caroline once told me how her roommate Shari had gotten engaged. The guy showed up at their door in a tuxedo and with a dozen long stemmed roses. Caroline obviously loved it. Roses, I thought. Great idea. Hold the thought.

Sometime in that season, my friends Stuart and Suzanne had a Friday night dinner at their house with Caroline and I. It was special. I squirmed the whole time. At one point, Stuart said to Caroline, "how many kids would you like to have one day, Caroline?" She looked at her plate as she said… "twelve."

"Twelve!" I burst out laughing. I told her I had been telling people that I wanted twelve kids. No answer.

After dinner, Stuart and Suzanne announced that they had to put the kids to bed and left us to do the dishes. I asked Caroline if she had ever thought she might be called to missionary work. Staring at the dishes, never looking up, she said simply, "Oh yes." I asked, has the Lord ever given you an idea where you might be serving. She still didn't look up. A pause. "Oh yes." I was puzzled by her reserve. "Well… where?"

"Africa."

I didn't laugh this time. I almost dropped the dish I was drying. I said quietly, "You know I want to be a missionary in Africa one day." "Yes," she said.

Later, I reproved my friends for trying to "set us up" via that Friday night dinner. Suzanne looked at me. "David, who was our guest last Friday night?" I had to think. "Mary." And who was our guest the previous Friday night?" "Ann." And who was our guest the previous Friday night?" Betty."

"David, we invite one of the single women in the church to dinner every Friday night, every one of them an old friend of mine. Why has Caroline had this effect on you?"

It was at this moment that Suzanne's husband Stuart asked if I had ever fasted and sought God as I said I would. "Oh Yes!" I said. "God said yes!" He seemed astonished. "You never said anything." I replied "What does it matter? She barely knows I exist so this will be a long season… but it is enough that I know." He seemed to choose his words carefully. "You should tell Pastor Mark so that he can be praying with you." I agreed. The next day I called the pastor's secretary and asked if I might have an appointment with Pastor Mark. Of course, she said, but he has left for the holidays and won't be back for three weeks. I'll get an appointment for you then. I said it was fine and there was no hurry.

Three weeks went by quickly. I asked for a long lunch break from my job at the university and took the Metro up to Capitol Hill. The church had an office on C Street SW and I met Pastor Mark there and we walked a few blocks to a lunch place he recommended.

After the pleasantries, I told him that I had been fasting and praying and that God had spoken to me (how oddly that rolled off my tongue as I had never said it before!) about Caroline Grabau. He looked thoughtful, as though he had never considered such a thing. I wondered if a fatherly correction would come now. "I can see that." He finally declared. "Debbie and I will pray with you." But he added that with my past, I owed it to her to have a full STD check-up before starting a relationship. "Take care of that and call me when you have the results." Smart man. I had not thought of it. In the years that have followed, I have told every young man about to be engaged that unless he is a virgin, he must, in honour, have a full scan before he starts a relationship. It would be utterly unfair to start a relationship, to ask for someone's heart, until one is able to divulge any long-term issues that it is within one's power to know.

Telling the parents

The next item on my checklist was to let my parents know that I was "involved" in a relationship, because if I were to be suddenly engaged without warning they might be confused… hurt… worried. I had not been able to go home for Christmas break due to my work schedule, so I scheduled a mid-January trip.

Arriving in my hometown, I stopped first at the ocean, kicked off my shoes, and trudged down to Porpoise Point. It was a Florida-cold January afternoon, meaning, not too cold but too cold for a swim. I thought of Caroline. I was excited to show her this place. I didn't know if she would get it… that my soul was drawn back here season after season, that nothing was real until I had thought it through at the sea.

I looked out into the ocean. I finally understood. This was how I had heard God's voice until now, in the greatness and majesty and peace of the sea. Here, I had been most intimate with God, though I hadn't known what I had felt. Now I knew a new way to hear him, and I could hear Him anywhere, even in the hustle and bustle of Washington, DC. I would always love the sea, but I would not need it as I had once needed it.

I enjoyed a long, restful week with my parents. On Friday, January 20th, we sat in the back tv room at my Grandmother Ruth's house and watched the inauguration of George H.W. Bush. I had let the week go by without mentioning the reason for my trip but now I had them all in one room.

"I wanted to tell you something," I began. "I've met a girl in DC… well actually I've known her a long time but I really think she's the one for me." My Mom was happy. "We are so excited." She said she knew that was why I had come to visit. I was deeply puzzled… how would she know? "A mother knows," is all she said.

They pummelled me with questions. In all my thoughts of this moment, I had not thought of what they might ask. In truth, I still barely knew Caroline Grabau and the facts of her life were way beyond me.

"Where is she from?" Gosh, was it Connecticut or Vermont? I settled for "New England."

"How old is she?" Silence. "About my age. She is definitely old enough to get married!"

"Where did she go to college?" "Um… somewhere up north." Good answer. To Southerners, everything north of Virginia was vaguely "up north."

"What kind of nursing did she study?" "Um… General stuff." I think. "Well, there are a lot of kinds of nursing, dear, my mom started. "What kind of nursing is she doing now?" Think. Think. I remembered her talking about the hospital.

"Hospital nursing!" I said triumphantly. I could see Mom had decided to let that go.

"Tell us about her family." Yes! I knew this one! "She lives with her sister. Her brother is a pastor in Williamsburg. Her mom still lives in Vermont. Her Dad is… um… actually, not really sure."

Grandma Ruth turned her head slowly to glance at Mom and Dad. Dad looked puzzled. I certainly didn't seem to know much about this girl. I dived into the real explanation.

"You see I prayed and asked God if she was really the one for me and I know God said yes."

Stunned looks.

"How did you know God said that?"

"What do you mean by, 'God said?'"

"Because God cares about the most important person in our life and he made someone for me so I knew that He would tell me if I just asked him. Also, I fasted."

It was just about over. Silence. "That's nice dear."

For the next two days they asked questions, and I could tell them just a bit more, but not much. Lots of scepticism in the air. Lots of polite talk.

Back to Washington

There was a January church conference that year and as it happened, Caroline had been sent by her employer that weekend to a Nursing Conference. At the church conference I had two items on my agenda, to make sure I saw David Grabau and to meet his fiancée, Maia. I found David at a reception, and we chatted happily, and he brought Maia to introduce me to her. We had a great time getting to know each other. A little later, I looked across the room and saw her talking to a friend and when she was done, she and her friend looked up at the same moment and looked directly at me, startling all three of us. Nervous hand waves. I wondered... I hoped... that Caroline was saying something to her family about me.

I will never forget one night at the conference when I was standing near the front of the room with hundreds of others, worshipping God and for me, as usual, thinking about Caroline. I suddenly realized a small girl was standing in front of me, looking into my face. I recognized her as the daughter of our most senior ministry's leaders, Evangeline. I said "Hello!" She said, "Hello. Are you married?" I said "No." She looked deep into my face. Then she concluded, "But you are about to be." I laughed. "Do you think so?" She nodded solemnly. "Yes." I picked her up and took her to her mother. When you are journeying with God, He sends little messages, little glimmers of hope, to encourage you on the way.

Being sure

There was one more thing on my list that January. I needed to get those tests done that the Pastor had urged me to do.

I was a student and went to a free clinic. They told me to call in three weeks. I didn't mind the wait. This was a long-term project. But when I called in three weeks they apologized and said the vials of blood I had contributed had shattered in the "spinner," which sometimes happens. They asked me to come and start over. I was discouraged. A part of me realized that this could be the piece to hamper my dreams and that in fact, I might be sick. I shared my discouragement with my friend Stuart. He was working for an OBGYN/midwife couple in our church. He said, "Just ask them to do it. I'll ask them if you like. I agreed. He asked them. They agreed. That day I submitted blood tests. A few days later our midwife friend called me back. "David there are no issues whatsoever. Your tests are clean."

I was astonished. I had convinced myself that with a past like mine, there would be a reckoning in the natural, however big or small. I hung up the phone and hung my head, thanking God for His mercy. Why was God so good to me? I know that in a fallen world, many people suffer for their sins and sometimes innocent people suffer for the sins of others. I was not innocent. I was a sinner already saved by grace but not free from consequences in the natural. His love and mercy worked on this occasion to suspend judgement in my life. To this day, I easily fight tears when I think about it.

Later I saw my friend Stuart and he asked me about the results. I told him they were all clear. As he knew my past, I fully expected him to be amazed and thoughtful as I was. Instead, he was all business. "Great. Call Pastor Mark tonight and tell him." It was Saturday night. Pastor Mark would be busy getting ready for church the next day. I said it could wait a week. He said, "No, Pastor Mark said to call him as soon as you knew. He would want to know. Call him."

I called him. I started by apologizing for calling him on a Saturday night, but he assured me it was fine. I told him that I had the results, and that God had been merciful. I was all clear. He was, oddly, all business, too.

That's great, he said. "Debbie and I have prayed, and we feel this is so right. Why don't you call Caroline and ask her out and share your heart with her? Ask her tomorrow morning."

It took my breath away. What could he be saying? I had been clear to him that she was in the dark, that she didn't know me at all yet. Why would I risk a sudden revelation that might scare her off? He just said, "I think it'll be fine."

Still holding the phone, I leapt up from the couch and grabbed my forehead. "Do you think that's a good idea!" He said, "I do!"

The first revelation in that season came from God. The second came from Pastor Mark. He had not told me, but I knew. He wouldn't push me to be so bold unless… was it possible?

Caroline had already said something to him or to his wife.

But what had she said? There's a guy and I think he is kind of cute? I sometimes wonder if this guy likes me. God has told me he's the One. That last possibility seemed impossible. But why wouldn't He speak to her so clearly?

He had done so with me! But she had barely spoken to me for the last two years and had only become friendly in the last two months. If she had ever had a thought about me, she had certainly concealed it.

And in an instant, I knew that I knew. Of course, she had concealed her feelings. Hadn't we been taught, men and women alike, not to pursue a spouse? Hadn't we been told a hundred times to let God wake-up the man and prepare the woman, and not to get in the way? Hadn't we been charged to be patient until we knew that we knew that we knew. If Caroline knew… she would have done her best to avoid me. And she certainly had avoided me.

I had a dream that night. In the dream, Caroline and I were passing in the hallway but this time, instead of avoiding me, she looked fully into my eyes and smiled. I knew that she knew.

Sunday 19 February

The next day… Sunday… was the day of my graduation from the George Washington University. Just a few days before I had made what I thought was a fairly bold invitation by inviting Caroline and her sister to my graduation. They said they couldn't because Liz had responsibilities at church, and it was Caroline's once a month weekend shift at the hospital. But Stuart and Suzanne had invited them and about 30 others to a graduation party at their house (where I lived in the basement apartment) for later in the afternoon, and they had both said yes to that.

Stuart, Suzanne and I plotted. I was determined to talk to Caroline the next day. After all, I now knew, and I was done waiting.

Suzanne's job was to get Caroline into the den under some pretext. I would come in and Suzanne would excuse herself. Perfect. I looked at the den and decided to bring a formal antique chair from my apartment that my grandmother had given me. Caroline would look great sitting there.

In the morning, my friends Dawson and Anne attended my graduation. They had a long trip to Florida in front of them that day and had tried to excuse themselves from the party afterward. I had said, "No, you have to come. It's not really a graduation party." Perplexed looks. "Well what kind of party is it?" "Please, just come." They did.

The house filled with college and church friends and lots of noise and laughter. Church team and students alike had grown close over the last two years, and everyone loved it when we had an excuse for a party. We were a happy crowd, but no one was happier that day than me and not because I had graduated.

At last, Caroline arrived. I can still see her entering the front door. She looked exhausted, her hair as though it had been under a surgery cap all day (it had) with no make-up all. She was beautiful. I was ecstatic. A few presents were opened, one from Caroline and Liz and their mother… a beautiful maroon leather briefcase. After a while, I saw Suzanne take Caroline to the den. I thought to myself, "It's time."

I waited just five minutes and tapped lightly at the door and said, "Suzanne?" She said, "Just a moment." I waited patiently. After a few moments, Suzanne came to the door and exited and I stepped in the room.

The tension was high, but we were both smiling. "Hi Caroline." "Hi David." I realized she was sitting on an old sofa in the corner instead of in the beautiful antique chair in the center of the room. Of course. She wouldn't take the best chair when Suzanne was with her. They had been sitting on the sofa.

"Before I say anything, I have a request."

"Yes"

"Would you mind sitting in that chair."

"Whatever you like."

As she crossed the room, I had a moment to reach into the closet. By the time she sat down and was facing me, I was holding an elegant box of long-stemmed red roses.

She literally gasped and put a hand to her mouth. I leaned forward and set the box in her lap as gently as though it were a newborn baby. We stared at them together, me sitting on the edge of a seat just a few inches from her.

This may have been the most challenging moment of my life. I was deeply in love with a girl I had never spoken to in any intimate way. It was time to share my heart with her.

I told her that since the day I first saw her at church on Sunday, 11 December, I had been completely taken with her and the great calling on her life. I told her how I had her on a pedestal so that even when I was really smitten with her, I had been afraid to tell anyone for fear of being rebuked because she was so out of my league. I told her how dizzy I felt after we spoke in her car the first time. I told her how my obsession with her had nearly ruined my academic standing. I told her that I thought more than once that I was losing my mind. I talked fast and hard until there was nothing left to say. From somewhere deep within I found and firmly declared the desire of my heart.

"I love you and I want you to be my wife one day."

There. It was done. If she replied with anything that sounded like "you do me great honour," I would have to run screaming from the house. It was done. If she said she would consider it and wasn't ready to talk, I would have been crushed. I had gambled it all. I had nothing left to offer above what I had already said. It was done.

Fortunately for me, she waited only a moment. It seemed like a very long moment. She did something she hadn't done in the many, many months she had been acting as though she didn't know my name: she looked me squarely in the eye. I saw shyness but I saw passion. I realized the moment was as hard or harder for her than it had been for me. Then she said gently,

"I love you and I want to be your wife one day." Emphasis was on the "be."

My heart pounded so fast. It was the happiest moment of my life. In the midst of the joy, I heard the Holy Spirit say, "Did you hear what she just said. She is not like any woman you have ever known. She isn't asking you to be someone to her. She just wants to come along with you." Deep peace and calm filled me. It was what I had always wanted. I wanted the one I loved to want to be with me. And she did.

Our bubble burst in an instant and her eyes darted to mine. "What are we going to do about all those people down there?" I grinned. "Let's go tell them."

I admit that I don't remember a lot of what happened next. We came into the room arm in arm. My friend Stuart shouted, "David and Caroline are engaged!" Lots of screaming. Lots of hugs. I looked across the room at her sister Liz who had a blank look on her face, then quietly walked straight to Caroline and began shouting over the crowd "When did this happen? We were just in the kitchen cleaning lettuce and you were not engaged!"

"It just happened Lizzie, In the den. In the last ten minutes."

Everyone was yelling to hear how and when this had happened. Finally, we sat in chairs in front of the fireplace. I told my story, much of which I had just told Caroline minutes before, but with much more detail. She gasped and laughed and shook her head and said, "I can't believe it."

Then it was her turn. It was my turn to laugh and cry and gasp and shake my head in disbelief.

Her story too was a God-story. In the days and weeks and months to follow, I learned how God had shaped and moulded Caroline Grabau.

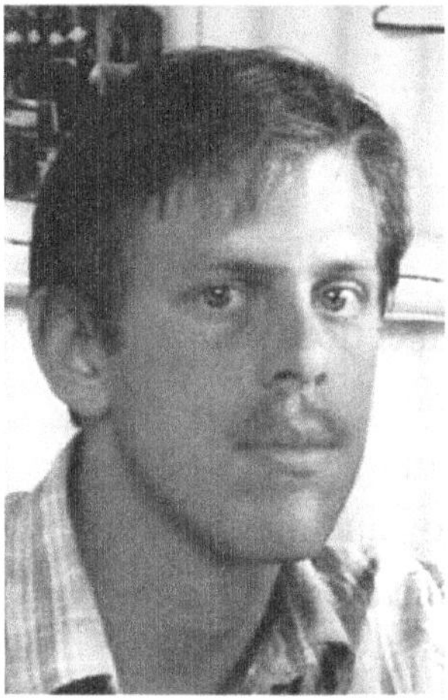

Caroline's Story

I grew up in a prosperous family in Connecticut and we had the home, the clothes, the good schools, the country club life of a well-to-do family. We were taught that looks were important. But I was a natural tomboy and did not fit in. I loved the outdoors and not the tea parties. I hated talking on the phone, where many girls spent hours. I loved sports, getting dirty, rough housing. I was a so-so student, not making the grades that might have gotten some respect from my peers. I felt I was the outsider. When I was 11, my parents divorced and like most children of divorce, I felt sure it was my fault.

During my teenage years, my mom began to help delinquent teenagers in our neighbourhood. They needed mothering and she was truly a mother out of legend. She could listen, advise, cry with the sad ones and laugh all night with the happy ones. She was generous to a fault and could cook and bake like a chef. These feral youth were welcome in our home at any hour.

But it was the 70's. I cannot tell you how quickly my family and our delinquent friends went from being "one big happy family" to lighting-up pot in the garage. Mostly unchurched, we had no standards, no morals, and no one to save us from ourselves. Mom went to bed earlier than us. Soon after, I became immoral.

It was the beginning of a very bad year.

When one of our new "friends" said, "Let's move to Vermont," we were all in. Mom was jaded, unhappy in a failed relationship that followed her divorce from my dad. She felt she didn't fit in as she once had with her social set and perhaps, she was beginning to seek meaning in her life.

Connecticut held very few attractions for me. We became a broken family there. I wondered if relationships were always short-term. I had a spinal condition that caused me to wear a brace for ten years that left me looking deformed and fat in even in the nicest clothes. Kids can be mean to disabled kids, and I fit into that category for a long season. By the time we left for Vermont, I was free of the brace and ready to start a new life.

I was 16 when my mother packed up our big Connecticut house and took my brother, sister and I and our new "family" to live in Vermont.

We had fun. We partied all night long with our new friends. We were rebellious, casual with drugs and alcohol and non-committal about morality. We knew a lot of people and everyone wanted to know us.

Rumours reached my father in CT that I was dating a "drugee" and that our home had become a drug-den. Only his threats to my mom to have us all removed from her care brought sudden, radical change. Then my exiled boyfriend began to stalk me.

Being stalked

Only a woman who has been stalked by a boyfriend can understand what happened next. Today, 40 years later, I still can't get my mind around how my boyfriend talked me into running away with him.

It was Christmas time. It was my favourite time of the year and when my family realized I had disappeared, they suddenly remembered that I had kissed each of them goodbye as I left the house. Not being much of a spymaster, I left a clear trail by leaving my car next to the bus station. My Mom had no trouble convincing the small-town ticket agent to tell her where I had gone. Danbury, Connecticut.

I did not really want to go. It broke my heart to leave and especially to leave at Christmas. I loved my family. I was so torn between my manipulative boyfriend and my disapproving family. But he could tell me anything and I believed him. I remember the mind game I played for two and half hours on the way to Danbury. I felt I was losing my mind. At last, the bus arrived. The bus doors swung open, and I expected to see my boyfriend.

I did see him. In handcuffs. But standing in front of him, waiting for me at the bottom of the steps, was my dad. Mom had called him.

I was so happy. I was so humiliated. I was so thankful. I was so embarrassed. I was relieved. I ran and hugged my dad and cried. I thanked him.

My boyfriend was a legal adult and I was a minor. In a search of his car, the police found illegal knives.

My boyfriend was arrested. I was sent home for Christmas.

Almost ruining everything

My boyfriend came back to Vermont a few months later, but I had time to see the destructiveness of my relationship with him. I was overwhelmed with shame and guilt over how I had behaved and who I had become. I began to believe my family and friends who told me he had other girlfriends. When he tried to lure me back in, God arranged for me to "catch him" with one of those girlfriends. I was heartbroken. But I was finished with him for good. It was done.

And still, the stalking continued. When he was angry, he would come to my house late at night and spin wheelies in the road in front of our house. My family was frazzled and scared and driven to distraction. One night, in our desperation, we almost ruined our lives forever.

My Mom concocted a scheme to send my ex-boyfriend to his grave. It involved a gun and a plan that she thought would keep us all out of jail afterward.

But once again, God intervened.

My mom later said that though she wasn't a Christian yet, God spoke to her that it wouldn't work and that she would end up in jail and her children would be raised in a delinquent home.

She screamed and called off the plan with minutes to spare.

My Mom was searching for meaning in her life and now, so was I. I will never forget standing on the bottom steps in our house talking to my mom who was standing in the foyer. We were looking directly into each other's eyes.

"What is life all about? Is there any meaning in life at all?" I said. "If this is all there is, why should we keep living?"

She shook her head and quietly said, "I don't know."

I am grateful there is no melancholy or suicidal tendency in our family as that night might have been our last. We were at rock bottom. We were ready for something to change.

Trying God

The next day, my take-charge mom found a newspaper and said, "Let's try a new church." We had, paradoxically, been churchgoers, but as you can see, we were still deeply troubled. She began to look at the local church ads and found a small CMA church. She said we should go there on Sunday. And we did.

I don't remember much about that service, but I distinctly remember the pastor saying that CMA missionaries from Southeast Asia would be visiting soon and he appealed for someone to host them. My Mom, ever the hostess, told the pastor afterward that we would be happy to be their hosts.

I wonder what he thought when the unsaved guests were the only ones in the congregation who offered to help. But we had a big, lovely house and that was exactly what was needed. God works in mysterious ways. He agreed to let us host them and that is how a beautiful Christian Missionary Alliance couple came to spend part of their furlough in our big Vermont home for a full week.

I often remember that my mom's heart to take care of people got us into the worst season of our lives, but then I remember that it was that same heart that God used to bring us to Him.

That week, we were forever changed.

Early in the week, they asked if we would like to see a slideshow of their work. I remember my mother pulling out an old projector and screen in preparation. In the next hour, they showed my brother and Mom and I (my sister was sick in bed) a slide show of their work in tribal villages, including the ministering of the Gospel. It was the look on the tribal people's faces that startled us. Before and after. Hopeless to joyful. Over and over. It was both who we were and what we wanted. Sunk in hopelessness. Yearning for Joy. We cried. We saw transformation in the faces on the slides. Our hearts were broken. We had tears in our eyes as we asked them what we were seeing. They told us how these people had asked

Jesus to forgive their sins and had invited Him into their lives and hearts.

We were ready. We asked if we could do that too. They prayed a simple prayer with us. We had lots to ask forgiveness for, but when we were done, we knew something had happened. Peace invaded us. Within a few days, my sister had prayed the same prayer.

Everything changed

We had thought we needed Vermont to make a fresh start. We realized that we just needed Jesus. We attended that church and its Bible studies. Our lives began to change… slowly. We began to feel uncomfortable with the old parties and the drinking.

After a season, Vermont became wonderful. There were a hundred moments when I thought, "this is exactly where I want to be. I fit here."

First, there were the mountains. The colours of autumn were a picture of heaven. I thought that God had a paint brush and had drenched the countryside with His favourite colours. I would stop the car often just to stare into the mountains. Deer and racoon crossed the road and made us slow down. Bears would growl in the night, reminding us that nature was close.

Each season was profoundly different. The freshness of spring, the rest of summer, the beauty of fall, the quiet of a snowy winter night.

Snow is wonderful. It helped me to understand in later years the Scripture that our sins would be white as snow. Really white snow is blinding in the day, but still lights up the countryside at night. It is like God's forgiveness, covering everything.

And then there were the cows. I began a lifelong love affair with cows. They were simple, homey, relaxed, slow-moving and made the sweetest, most comforting sounds.

I learned to ski and then to snowmobile. In winter I took the snowmobile to school. Every Thursday I went skiing. The kids at my school were mostly country kids and loved to ski and snowmobile and explore the woods, just like me. My simpler heart was appreciated. I didn't need to make the grade to become President of my class. My school was one tenth the size of my former school. I knew the name of everyone in my class. I was a person. Everyone knew my name, too. I wore overalls, work boots and flannel shirts. They were perfect for the country life. My dresses and heels gathered dust from neglect.

Jesus had healed me, and he was using Vermont to be part of the healing. I never wanted to leave.

I didn't want a lot in life, just to be married after high school and to have babies shortly thereafter. Many girls have a "Hope Chest" to prepare for getting married by collecting linens and household items. I started my Hope Chest as a teenager and by my early twenties it had expanded to a "Hope Basement" in my mother's house where I collected furniture and appliances. One day I was at a country store in my hometown in Vermont and saw a queen-size 4-poster bed that I loved. I was a nurse by then and making a good salary. I bought it. I worried briefly that I would marry someone who hated it, but I shrugged my shoulders and said, "Oh well, we can always sell it." It went into the Hope Basement, fully wrapped, for several years, with matching dresser.

Eventually I accepted a proposal of marriage from a dear family friend, a really nice young Vermont guy who I knew could help me stay in the country life I loved.

Rounding a corner I never saw coming

But a tornado was about to descend on my life. And it all started with Keith Green.

Christian singer and evangelist Keith Green died in a plane crash on 28 July 1982. His wife Melody fulfilled their concert plans with the "Keith Green Memorial Concerts," where over 300,000 people in 110 cities heard a huge, on-screen Keith give a call to missions. His song, "Jesus commands us to go" broke my heart. Keith later preached, "He has already commanded us to go. We need a word to stay, not a word to go."

I vowed to God that I would go. I felt Him add, "to Africa."

Back at home, I knew that everything was different. Would I really choose my preferred life by marrying my fiancée and planning a quiet life in Vermont, especially after the encounter I had just had with God? For some time, I successfully quieted my fears. There would be a way to do it all, I was sure.

When my brother and sister moved to Washington DC and went to a great church there, I could see they were growing up in the Lord, and I knew that I was not! There was a faith and a zeal and a focus for God and His Kingdom that I had never seen in them. I wanted that, too! For the first time, I began to want something more than a husband, babies and Vermont. My soul was restless. What was it? Much later, I realized that all I really wanted was to know God's will for my life, and to do it!

It is hard when you have everything you want but know that it is not what God wants for you. I could get married and have my first baby within a year. Or I could pursue Him and wait for His timing. I chose a compromise. I would go to DC for one year. I felt I would grow more in that one year than I would in twenty if I stayed home in Vermont. My fiancée was not happy. "If you go, you'll never come back." I told him that was silly, but in my most private thoughts, I began to wonder if he was right.

I knew that God had it all for me… husband, children, ministry. I had such a strong sense that He was asking me to just obey and trust Him. But leaving would be tearing away from everything I ever wanted in the natural… a country town, New England, snowy winters, mountains… a simple life. Leaving was the hardest thing He could ask. But I suspected that everything I really wanted was on the other side of my obedience… on the other side of the mountains… on the other side of the world.

In Jerusalem there is a gate called "The Eye of the Needle" Gate. It is low and narrow. A camel packed with goods cannot get through. A camel would have to be unpacked to go through that gate. There could be no cargo. "Again I tell you, it is easier for a camel to go through the eye of a needle than for someone who is rich to enter the kingdom of God." Matthew 19:24

I felt rich. I had a loving home and a fiancé and had lived a truly happy life in Vermont for many years.

And then one day God showed me: Vermont had not healed me. He had healed me. And now He wanted me to go.

I struggled for a long time, but the answer was always clear. I had to let Him handle this.

Adding to my distress in that season was the realization that I would have to move to a big city. I hated cities. I had sworn never to live in one. I was sure that God would never ask that of me!

But He did.

And so, I packed my little car and drove out of the sanctuary of my mother's home and the mountains of Vermont. I was heartbroken. But I kept thinking that if I could leave Vermont, I could obey God to go absolutely anywhere.

I urged my fiancé to come live near me. After a while he came for a season. We hated city life together but at least we belonged to a great church, and we were growing. At some point we could see that our relationship had changed. Our lives were not about each other anymore. We each needed to pursue God and we both knew it.

At one point I excitedly signed up to go on a 6-week missions' trip to Africa! It was my sister who reminded me that the outreach was over my planned wedding week. I was nonchalant about the "scheduling issue." "So, we'll go together… or maybe we'll be married afterward." To my fiancé, it was final evidence that my heart had turned. He quietly told me one day that he was moving back to

Vermont. We both knew it was the right thing. I am glad to say that he and I and our families have been friends ever since.

Loving God more than ever, learning to obey Him no matter what… it was a season of tremendous growth. The only problem was that I was 26, single and without children.

I tried to wear my overalls and boots to church. My sister helped me to see the obvious… that I was trying NOT to fit in too much, as I was plotting to go home to Vermont. She helped me to create a new, city wardrobe. Everyone said I looked great. It just made me sad. But I knew I couldn't obey God halfway. I needed to throw myself into this new life.

One day I heard a sermon about living life as a single and not waiting for marriage to begin living life. I knew there was something I had not given up.

The final surrender

Soon after, I rented a truck and travelled to Vermont. I moved my "Hope Basement" to the home I shared with my sister and other ladies in the church in Virginia. It was the end of the small-town life I had dreamed of for myself. I had given it all up to God. The camel was unloaded. I was going through alone.

But there was no husband in sight and no sense of hope when I pulled up to my Virginia townhouse to unload the truck. I cried many tears. I enjoyed having all my furniture and household goods surrounding me, but they were a constant reminder that I had given up the last shreds of the life I had tried to create with a husband. I had sacrificed it. God had asked me to give it all up and I was obedient. I had let my Hope Basement, the symbol of married life coming, to become… furniture. The bed was just a bed now. At that moment, there was only melancholy.

I dutifully went about unpacking the boxes and furniture.

I will never forget what happened next.

God speaks

It was a Saturday, and I had just unpacked the last of my goods, my beautiful four-postered bed. I had started to make it for the first time, stretching fine linens across the unused mattress. I bought these sheets and this bed for my wedding night but God had said to let it go and I had let it go, in my heart and in the natural. It was just a bed now and I would enjoy it. The sun shone through the basement windows, the bedroom I had chosen in this house.

In the quiet, I heard God's voice like a whisper:

"In one year, I'll tell you who you will share this bed with."

I was startled. I stopped, standing next to the bed. I knew this was not my thought. I was not looking for "payback" from God! I had given everything to God because He asked for it and I wanted to please Him.

The goodness of God. He had decided to bless me in my obedience with a promise, straight from His heart to mine. The kindness of God saw my aching soul and decided to bless me with the gift of hope.

Hoping and waiting

There were some great guys in the church. I wondered about one or two of them. Wondering can be a slippery slope for a single woman. A longing heart goes down that trail easily.

But this new promise from God was becoming the greatest adventure of my life. Could I continually seek God in the midst of my unfulfilled wants? I heard His voice asking me every day… what do you want? Me or a husband? I was afraid sometimes that it was an either/or question!

But I knew that it wasn't an either/or question… not in my case. I had such a sense that on the brink of giving me the desires of my heart, He wanted me to know that life was all about Him. It was not about a husband. It was not about children.

I had to learn to take my emotions as well as my thoughts captive (2 Cor 10:5). Every day for months I sought Him. I read my Bible and meditated and slowly, in the storm of my emotions, God brought peace and perspective. I had to learn to wait, to let God order my steps. It was an inner fight.

What is waiting on God? I learned that it is not like waiting for dinner or even for Christmas. There is no sitting in an armchair about it. It's an inner battle to wait well. It is a battle to not be discouraged or cynical or doubtful or ungrateful, whether you're waiting for God to give you a husband or a child or to fulfil any other promise. You are in a battle to become the Godly person who will hear "Well done" on the right day.

For a woman of marrying age, it is a battle to avoid all the wrong ones out there. There are plenty of them. There are guys who have no heart to wait and are relying on their charm and boldness and good looks to win you. Whether it is one of these guys or just a great guy in the church, it is a battle not to become distracted every time a guy is nice to you.

It is a battle to purify your faith. It is about waiting for what you know in faith is coming long before you see it (Heb 11:1-6).

God grew me up in this season. He wasn't just growing me up to be ready for marriage, although that is what first drove me to Him. I needed so much more faith for the years and decades ahead. First, I would need faith for a husband and children. I would need faith to see our children follow Him. I would need faith to move to Africa. I would need faith for the many other children I knew were being sent to me. I needed to win this battle first to be a woman of faith for our calling, for all the children who were coming, for Africa.

In this season I read Derek Prince's book, "God is a Matchmaker." He is still one of my heroes of the faith. I was amazed. What God took Derek through on his way to marrying his wife Ruth was in many ways what I was going through. God was purifying Derek long before he married Ruth. I became certain that God was preparing me for marriage. I was 27. In one year, I would have been waiting 10 years for a husband. But I became convinced that God has a timetable. As with the biblical Adam, my husband would be ready when I was ready, not before. God knew what He needed to do in my heart and in my husband's heart to make us ready. I made up my mind to hope and to wait.

A potluck dinner

A year after the God-moment while making my bed, the church held a Saturday night potluck. I loved these moments as I loved cooking, washing dishes, playing with children and fellowship. As I walked out of the kitchen doors into the dining hall, my eyes suddenly focused on a guy in the church I had seen but didn't really know. He was bouncing a baby against his chest and whispering to him to get him to be quiet. My heart began pounding. There were three Davids in the church and I knew he was one of them, but that is all. My heart melted. Where is my husband who, I knew, would love my children like that guy does?

Later that night, as we were cleaning up, my eyes turned, and I saw a guy on his hands and knees scrubbing a messy spill on the floor. My heart almost stopped. Same guy. I said to my sister and other friends, "Get a load of that guy. Have you ever seen a single guy do that?" My sister said, "That's David Webb."

I wondered why it affected me so much, but I could easily go down an emotional trail with a guy, so I made up my mind to get a hold of myself and stay focused on my relationship with God. But I kept wondering why I felt so affected by those two snapshots. Holding the baby, of course, bought into all my desire for children. But cleaning up the floor? Then I realized why I was affected… he had a servant's heart. He was clearly used to taking care of things AND taking care of people. No doubt that was the kind of guy I wanted to marry. The kind of guy? The guy? And then I knew I needed to stop. I was going down a trail that I had been down before. I was after God's heart now, not after a husband.

I tried. I made up my mind not to think about him. Still, I found myself pressing my sister as casually as I could for details about him. Not much. Raised Catholic. From Florida. Studying at GW. Has an admin job. That disappointed me. I had always thought I'd marry a country guy, someone who would be good with his hands… a carpenter, a construction guy.

Nonetheless, I began to obsess. I did it quietly, but I was thinking about him all the time. I pretended I was excited about church events but really only if David was there. I was happy if I saw him, sad if I didn't. Finally, I told the Lord that He had to deliver me or tell me that David Webb was the one.

What happened next was not just about "getting a word" or "deciding." In the constant seeking of Him, I came to a profound moment of reaffirming that I really wanted God more than I wanted a husband. I realized that marriage was not going to make me whole. Only He could do that. I knew that I wanted Him more than I wanted David. The peace was indescribable. I knew that HE loved me and it would always be enough.

Being sure

With that foremost in my mind, I asked God to tell me about David Webb or to take away every thought of Him. I can't say when the answer came, but in the weeks after, somehow, I just knew. I knew that I knew, as we used to say in our church, in perfect peace and confidence that someday David Webb and I would be married. But that was not the most important thing that happened in that season. I was intimate with God. He was my first husband (Isaiah 54:5). God would add David to my life as well.

We were taught in our church that when you began to think of marrying, you should start by sharing your heart with your leaders, so I told my home cell leaders. They asked a lot of questions. I told them everything. I told them my disappointment that he was an office guy who wore a suit each day and not a construction worker. They laughed. And they promised to pray with me. I knew that at some point they talked to our pastors Mark and Debbie Caulk because Mark said to me quietly one day that they were praying with me. I knew why.

I learned from my friends that David had spent time serving in Africa and wanted to return there. Africa. My heart leapt back to the Keith Green Memorial Concert. I had told God I would go. He had told me that I would go to Africa.

I found out that the word was out among the girls of the church that David was telling people he wanted 12 kids. Was that possible? That is what I had been telling people since I was sixteen.

I knew what I had to do. For the sake of my future, for the sake of the marriage I believed was coming, in honour to David and to the Lord God. There was something I had to do.

I avoided him.

I avoided him like the plague.

I was not going to be the one to tell him that I was the one for him. He would have to hear from God himself. Women know how to let men know they are interested. I never wanted to wonder in all the years to come, or for him to wonder, if I had "lured him in." We as women have an ability to do that. I had done that before, but now I was forever changed. I was God's daughter. If God could speak to me, He could speak to David. And He would have to because I would have no part of that sacred moment.

And so I waited. Every workday morning, I passed the street where David lived on my way to work. I would throw a hand of authority in his direction and yell out the window, "Speak to him, Lord! Wake him up! Get him ready! Prepare Him!" The months passed.

The conference

Our church was in charge of Children's Ministry at a regional conference, and I was in charge of children's church. Every member signed up for a shift, including David. I was nervous about seeing David and hoped I wouldn't run into him. As I walked into the hotel, he was standing there, facing the front door. "Hi Caroline!" God knows me. He knew I actually just wanted to see David.
I will never forget the night David was serving in Children's Church and I did my rounds to check on all the

workers. David was to be sitting with 6 kids in a hotel room with another volunteer.

I knocked on the door and David promptly answered, bouncing a toddler on each hip and with a room full of children behind him. I thought, "Jesus help me to act normal!" He was calm, collected… like every day was a day he might babysit twelve kids. There were twelve children in the room! "Oh my goodness! Where's your helper?" "I don't know… they didn't show up. But it's ok." And it really was ok. The children were calm, playing and watching television. As much as I wanted to say, "I'll just stay and help," I knew this was way too many kids in one room.

I said, "I'll take the girls back to my room." He said he would walk me as far as the elevator where he would be within sight and hearing of the room full of boys. As we were walking to the elevator, he suddenly said, "This is just like your prophecy, Caroline." What prophecy?

"You know, the one where Pastor Mark said you have the heart of a mother, that you have the heart that Jesus had when He said, 'Suffer the children to come unto me,' that he gave you that heart because many, many children are coming to you, first in the natural, then in the spiritual."

I was stunned. That was… perfect. Even I couldn't have repeated that prophecy. I looked at him and looked away. How could he remember that? He smiled and waved as the elevator doors closed. I was emotionally wrecked. I had been nervous about coming to this conference because I was afraid that I would not be able to act in a normal way around David. And now this.

I decided to tell my sister because she could help me be sane and would pray with me. I could not believe the story she relayed. Her first conversation with David was after a church meeting on a DC Metro, some years before. She felt she knew that night that he was the one for me. I could not believe it. Lizzie and I were very close, but she had said nothing. But then I understood her dilemma. If this were from God, she was not going to get in the way.

Lizzie told my mother, who told my brother David, and my conviction became a tight-knit family secret. After six months, my brother said I needed to sign-up to be a part of whatever David was doing in the church. I remembered that a month before, they had put out an appeal for church members to be a part of the weekly campus Bible study at GWU. I got up my nerve and called David. He was so polite. He said thank you, but so many people signed up and started coming when we made that appeal. Better you stay serving at Children's Church! I was crushed. He clearly had not noticed me yet. He was still asleep. Oh Lord, help me!

Helping at Bible Study

Fortunately, his co-worker Laurie caught wind that I wanted to help and told me to come. She needed help with the ladies.

And that was how I got to know David. I could watch him teach, watch him lead discussion, laugh, frown, sing (in a group). I could unabashedly stare at him for 45 minutes once a week. I thought how easily he got along with international people. It was life to my soul. He is really cute!

Then one night he mentioned that he would take the DC Metro home because he didn't have his car. Anxiety gripped me. Would it be forward to offer him a ride? I came to the conclusion that he was basically just a brother who needed a ride and I had a car. I gave rides to so many people. This was not out of character. I offered to take him home. He accepted.

It was easier than I thought. We talked about the Bible study and found it easy to "get" each other, to agree, to discuss the Lord we loved. It was as though we had chatted a thousand times before. It was magic.

And then there was "the look."

I had been taught that when you drive people to their home, you wait for them to get to the door before driving away. I couldn't actually see his door, far down the driveway and around a corner, but I waited till he got to the top of the driveway. Suddenly he turned around and looked at me. It was "The look." It was as though we saw each other for the first time. We stared for a moment into each other's eyes. We waved goodbye enthusiastically.

All the way home, I sang and praised God. Something had happened.

I enjoyed Bible studies more than ever. I would look for David's car as I arrived. If it was not there, I was happy. He needed a ride.

About that time, my sister told me that I really needed to alert my dad, who might not understand if I went from "no boyfriend" to "engaged." It was awkward. I told him that there was a guy that I thought might be the one and I wanted to give him warning. I told him about the master's degree, being a Davidson College grad, working at GW. There wasn't much else. I didn't know much else.

He said, "Was that the guy who took your coat when we arrived at church that time?" I was baffled. When? Then I remembered. He was right. It was David. David was on the usher team and usually took my coat. I couldn't believe that Dad remembered him. He said, "He seems like a nice guy."

One night at church, my home cell leader who I had first talked to about David came running to me excitedly. “Caroline, David’s last job was as a carpenter with a construction company. Stuart says he is a natural handyman. He is exactly what you hoped for.” God knew the desires of my heart!

In December, my roommates and I had a carolling party that started at our house. David said he was sick but wanted to come for a little while. He arrived, looking very sick. I didn’t care how sick he was. I was so glad he came. But all too soon it was time to go carolling. He said he had better stay back and wait for everyone to return. He explained that he had been fasting and praying all week and woke up sick that morning and had to skip church but had had a great prayer time. He smiled at me. I thought up an excuse to stay. He was my guest, and I needed to get him settled with a hot drink and snacks. I did that, but afterward, I could think of no reason to continue standing awkwardly near him except that I wanted to be with him, with all my heart. I made my excuses and slipped away.

I was a little down that New Year’s Day started without an engagement. One day I had an odd call from Pastor Mark. Do you still feel David Webb is the one you are going to marry? I instantly said Yes.

He said, "Do you like surprises?" "Umm… yes…" He said "OK" and hung up. That was too little information. I barely slept.

The graduation party surprise

David asked me quite late if I wanted one of the three tickets to his graduation. I was deflated that I could find no one to take my nursing shift that weekend and I had to say no. At least there was a graduation party afterwards, and Lizzie and I would definitely be there.

I remember showing up at the party late and tired, but glad for another chance to see David and dream. Our friend Suzanne asked me to come to the den because she wanted to talk to me about something. We chatted about… nothing, really. And then there was a knock at the door.

She said, "That's David. He wants to talk to you."

"To me?" All alone, I thought. My heart began to pound.

Suzanne exited and David entered. He closed the door and leaned his back against it, facing me. He smiled and said, "Hi Caroline." I smiled and said, "Hi David."

He glanced around the room. "Before I say anything, would you mind sitting over here?" I would have done anything he asked at that moment, and I was not going to ask why. As I slipped into the comfortable antique armchair and turned around to face him, my heart completely melted. He was facing me, standing upright in his Sunday-best suit, holding an elegant box of long-stemmed red roses.

He handed them to me. He sat in the chair close to me with his hands touching mine and began to tell me the most amazing things… how he had noticed me and wondered about me and fallen in love with me.

Could this be real? Jesus, YOU did it. YOU told him and I didn't! Did I really run this race of faith? What I never saw in the natural was real life in front of me! David was asking me to be his wife. I was undone!

It was all I had ever wanted… to be with him. And finally, I was. When he said he wanted me to be his wife one day, I could at last look him in the eyes and tell him the desire of my heart. "I want to be your wife one day."

I was glad that I didn't know in advance that God would ask me to wait until I was 29 for a husband. I am afraid I may not have had the courage to wait, preferring a second-rate marriage to God's choice for me. God wanted so much better for me.

After the party

David

After our astonished friends left my graduation party with hugs and kisses, Caroline wanted to call her mother. I said, "Why don't you let me call her?" I called her. "Mrs Grabau, this is David Webb calling from Washington DC, how are you tonight?"

"Well fine, David, how nice to hear from you."

"Mrs Grabau, I'm calling to ask your permission to begin dating Caroline with the intention of marrying her. Would that be all right with you?"

Screams of laughter. "Oh David that would make me very happy! Yes! Yes!" I said, "Thank you so much! Here's Caroline."

But some things had escaped me in the natural… the one drawback in our slow dance to get to know each other and to find the will of God, was that I was often clueless about the basic facts of her life.

I had heard much about Caroline's mother and brother and sister. I had not heard much about her father. I had wrongly thought he was not a part of their lives.

Then Liz said, "Should we call Dad now?" I looked at Caroline. Caroline said, "No, let me talk to him first. He'll be happy but he ordered me to never have a young man ask for my hand in marriage." Whew. I was off the hook. I could have made a mistake if I had asked Dad first, but God knew.

Getting to know each other

The next day, Caroline asked me to come to her house for dinner. Her work day ended a few hours before mine so she had time, she said, to make a home cooked meal. I remember stopping by my apartment to get showered and dressed (it was, after all, our second date), and looking in the mirror when a thought struck me. What if she's a terrible cook? Well, I will have to be polite, encouraging and truthful… I'll just have to figure it out. I said good-bye to my friends, Stuart and Suzanne, and told them I had already decided what to say in case of the worst. What worst, they asked? "If she's a terrible cook." They just said good-bye.

Apparently, after I left, Suzanne ran to the phone to call her friends to share this astonishing news. "He doesn't know! David doesn't know that Caroline is an amazing cook! He doesn't know her at all!"

That night, Caroline treated me to homemade chicken cordon-bleu with wild rice and fresh green beans sautéed in butter and almonds. The dinner rolls were also home-made. Dessert was homemade apple cobbler with ice cream. I really could not believe it. How had she whipped this up in such a short time? Brownies were not her only expertise.

Caroline told me that for three nights after our engagement, she stayed awake virtually the whole night, sleepless with wonder. She was not wondering that she was engaged. She was overwhelmed that she had obeyed God and waited for Him without interfering. She had run this race of faith in her heart and won it. She had actually heard from God all that she thought she had heard.

I also learned in the weeks after, that after I spoke to my friend Stuart about Caroline the first time, some months before, He rushed to a phone to call his wife. "It's happened. David has finally noticed Caroline Grabau."

I learned that after I spoke to pastor Mark, he went back to his office and called his wife Debbie. "David Webb came to talk to me about Caroline Grabau. It's finally happened."

I am still thankful to God for the character of all those involved that no one tried to "wake me up" in the wrong season. I was not ready. God was not ready to trust Caroline to me. When He was ready, He shook me gently and said, "It's time. Wake up." I had the pleasure of telling many people that I was engaged who, much to my surprise, said they had always assumed that Caroline and I would marry one day. None of them had said that to me.

Apparently, I was one of the last in our circle to understand what God was doing. First, Liz (who thought on the night she spoke with me on the Metro that I was the one for Caroline), followed by Caroline (fourteen months earlier!), then by half a dozen pastoral couples and last of all, by me.

Early revelations

Every day I revelled in the miracle. God had spoken to me, I had heard. I was getting married not only to a girl I was in love with but one who loved me and was made for me.

Made for me. There was much discussion about this point in our church. The easiest interpretation of the phrase is, "will be like me." We learned that nothing could be further from the truth.

In our case, some of our differences were somewhat stark. I loved literature. My taste ran from English romantic literature to American transcendentalism with a dose of Robert Frost and F. Scott Fitzgerald. In my Davidson College days, I decided that what I needed was a wife who shared this passion. I pictured us sitting by a fire on cold nights, reciting beloved passages to each other, querying each other on deeper meanings. I used to say it was the only quality I was sure I would find in my wife.

Caroline had passed high school English and vowed never to take an English class again.

Caroline came from a very sporty family. She herself was a whiz at touch football and was as strong as many of her brother's friends. Her brother once said that Caroline was the best brother a guy could want. Her beautiful mother was even stronger. Her father and grandfather were high school and college football players. Her grandfather Skeet Mayer was the star captain of the Tennessee Volunteers in the early 30's. Her family had season tickets to the New York Giants.

I had played a little football and threw the shotput in high school and never since. The only games I had watched since high school were my brother's college football games. I was not what she expected.

We learned that much of what we had put together in our minds based on likes and dislikes mattered very little. The adage "opposites attract" carries weight, too.

What was our answer when we discovered our differences? At first, we laughed about them. But in the long run, we found ourselves changing. I learned that I actually love spectator sports. Over the years, I became addicted to a few. Later, I would learn that watching my children play sports was the happiest way to spend a day. Or I would spend a happy day with a book at the ski lodge while Caroline went snow skiing.

On our honeymoon, I took along a book of poetry, "Sonnets from the Portuguese," to read to Caroline. I knew there were some lines that were not easy to understand, so as I read, I explained. I remember a beautiful meadow on Cape Cod where we had a picnic lunch and where I first introduced her to Browning. She listened and asked many questions.

And then it hit me like a thunderbolt. I had thought I wanted a wife who would read to me but what I really wanted was a wife who would let me read to her. Caroline was that woman. She loved to have things explained to her. In her simplicity and humility, she was ready to ask questions and push me to discover the deeper parts that I didn't really understand. She was perfect for me.

Perfect for me

In some marriages, this phrase means, "we fought like cats and dogs and improved each other tremendously." This too, is a valid meaning of "perfect for me." Some people mean, "my spouse drove me to my knees until I learned patience and forgiveness." This too is an example of "perfect for me."

What was really important in the way of similarities? We learned that loving God before marriage and serving Him together afterward was a recipe for a happy marriage. We have seen many examples of couples submitting to Christ only after marriage and it can work… but it is harder and takes a toll on the individuals and on the marriage first. Young men and women who set their hearts for God before marriage have a huge head start. We learned that being Christians committed to a relationship with Christ and already in agreement to look for direction in Him and in the Bible have already created a safe haven for marriage.

Three months after our declarations at my graduation party, Caroline and I made use of a long weekend to drive to Florida so she could meet my parents and grandmother and a brother and a sister. We were late arriving, so at the last minute we aborted taking the longer "Beach Road" that would have taken us by the beach. It was an easy weekend. Caroline charmed them as she charms almost everyone she meets, effortlessly.

As we said goodbye to my parents at the end of the weekend on the front porch of the home where I grew up, my mom whispered into my ear, "I'm so glad you found her. She's perfect for you." I saw her whisper something to Caroline, too. Afterward, I asked Caroline what my mom had said. "She said I was perfect for you."

Despite our differences with our parents, they often know us better than we think. I will always be grateful for my mother who let us know up front that as far as she could see, this was perfect.

As we left St Augustine, we took the long road and stopped by the beach. It was a calm sunny day. I was happier with who was beside me than I was with the beauty of the sea. I thought, "I can find God anywhere now." We pushed on, to Washington.

Epilogue

The topic of how a Godly person finds their spouse evokes passionate feelings. One need only do an internet search to find teachings and counter-teachings of the true "right way" to find a spouse. I have read angry denunciations and mockery of the way we came together and bitter diatribes against people who did not do it the way we did it. One young Christian wrote a book denouncing dating and swearing off anything but miraculous engagement and marriage. He later rejected his own teaching and left his church.

I promise you this: every Christian marriage is designed to be a miracle of grace. I have the greatest sympathy for those who found that their marriage became a disaster. God did not intend that.

But no two ways of finding a spouse are just alike.

At one extreme, some cultures will say that only a traditional engagement by going through others is a Godly way. At the other end, some suggest that if it doesn't feel relaxed and natural and deeply personal then there is something weird about it and it must be shunned. Neither contains the full wisdom of God. No one way boxes Him in and declares His purpose. He is vast. He can put people together any way He likes.

I know that God puts families together (Psalm 68:6 and John 19:26-27.) If he counts the hairs on our heads, and he does (Luke 12:7), then a matter as weighty as our lifelong partnership is definitely within his attention. He knew us before the foundation of the world (Jeremiah 1:5). Surely, he knew who was to be next to us on that journey.

That is why we believe that the grace of God will bring people together, regardless of their cultural norm.

For those who, like Caroline and me, had a checkered past and many relational failures, the way we did things was… perfect. It started with our seeking the Lord first (Matthew 6:33). It enabled us to lean fully on a Father God whom we deeply trusted and to put our personal feelings aside, and to include Christian friends and leaders whose opinion we deeply valued. For us… it was perfect.

In the decades since we married, we have discovered the many ways we "fit" each other. We not only fit well together as 30-year olds. We each became someone else in each decade that followed and still, we continue to be just right for each other. It is a recurring miracle. We couldn't have seen how we would change but God knew every season to come and He had them all in mind when he put us together.

We are sure of this… Faith pleases God (Hebrews 11:6). The more we are able to trust Him with the great moments of our lives, the more He will come through for us. We know this is not really David and Caroline's story. It is a story of God and how he took two messed up people and took over.

Rest assured, God will come through for you if you seek Him with an open and humble heart. He loves you. He cares about you. He knows every moment of your history that would cause you not to be full of rest in Him. He is full of love and kindness and wants the best for you. This will never change. If there is only one way you feel comfortable in pursuing a spouse, we believe He will meet you on that road, if you will let Him, as long as your seeking is not with hidden motives of lust, greed or selfishness.

Trust in the Lord who began a good work in you and he will complete that work as you trust Him. Let Him change you.

And remember… there is so much grace in God.

We discovered that the best gauge of a couple's suitability is their life's calling. We see the drawback there, as many people will discover their life's calling after they are ready to be married so matching the people and the calling is not easily done. And so, we fall back again on the grace of God. There are things about your spouse that will draw you even before your calling is clarified. Caroline caught a glimpse of my servant's heart and my ease with children. I caught a glimpse of her giftedness with children and her depth in talking of God and the Christian life. In each case, our hearts were stirred.

Today at home in Africa

You may wonder what we taught our own children and what we teach the many children we serve at the homes we operate in Africa.

We share our story with them, exactly as you have just read it. Our favourite moment is when we have young guests around our dinner table and someone asks, "How did you meet?" Occasionally, one of our own children will say, "Why don't you tell them how you met," then sit back with a twinkle in their eye. Once started, it is hard for us to stop. Consequently, our children have not only heard this story repeatedly but can chip in with parts we have forgotten.

We tell them that our dream is that each of them will have a story better than ours!

We taught them that it matters what families you spend your life with. Best of all is if your natural family and your spiritual family are the same, with church life and family life intertwined. And your friends really matter, too. "The righteous choose their friends carefully (Proverbs 12:26)." A popular adage is, "Show me your friends and I will show you your future."

Do we teach them to run when they sense attraction to someone? No. But we teach them that going slowly in matters of the heart is always wise. We teach them that much early dating is badly motivated and full of pitfalls of sexual confusion and failure and unnecessarily hurting people. We teach them that group dates and serving at church are excellent ways to get to know someone. We teach them that after deciding to be a Jesus-follower, this will be the most important decision of their life. It will affect them every day of their life. It will determine the happiness and stability of their home. It will influence generations who will come after them. Hurrying is not appropriate. As the Swahili people say, "Haraka, haraka, haina Baraka" (Hurrying, hurrying, brings no blessings).

Most importantly of all, we taught them one rule:

Get married when you know that you know that you know that God is putting you together with a certain person. We have the ability to seek God and to discern His voice. Sometimes that seems to take forever. Is that due to our weakness in hearing or due to His delaying an answer? Either way, the beauty is that the seeking and the waiting can draw you closer to God and makes you the spouse you want to be for your partner.

We c... all single people: Seek God. Wait on God. Slee ... be married, as it is for alm ... He is on the job. God has son

I h ... One. I sit with her on our ve ... ouble doors open into our b ... ountry bed that Caroline b ... des ago. From here we gaze i